FANTASTIC BEASTS
THE CRIMES OF GRINDELWALD

THE
ORIGINAL SCREENPLAY

WIZARDING
WORLD

J.K. ROWLING

FANTASTIC BEASTS THE CRIMES OF GRINDELWALD

THE ORIGINAL SCREENPLAY

ILLUSTRATIONS AND DESIGN
BY
MINALIMA

ARTHUR A. LEVINE BOOKS
AN IMPRINT OF SCHOLASTIC INC.

Library of Congress Control Number: 2018954211

ISBN 978-1-338-26389-3

10 9 8 7 6 5 4 3 2 1   18 19 20 21 22

Printed in the U.S.A. at LSC Communications in Harrisonburg, Virginia
First edition, November 2018

MIX
Paper from
responsible sources
FSC® C132124

To Kenzie

CONTENTS

FOREWORD

I've worked with many writers, but no one quite as special as Jo. She knows her characters and her universe inside out, she's one of the most dynamic thinkers I've ever met, and for someone who has enjoyed so much success she is incredibly grounded. Her storytelling is singular, yet she approaches the filmmaking process as producer and screenwriter with a genuinely collaborative spirit.

I first read *Fantastic Beasts: The Crimes of Grindelwald* in the spring of 2016, a full year and two months before we began shooting the film. The script felt layered, emotional, and that most precious of things: itself. For a filmmaker it offered many gifts and a huge sandpit in which to play. Whether the thrill of recreating Paris in the late 1920s, wrangling a new collection of wonderful beasts, or exploring an emotional, multistranded story with compelling characters and themes, each day of prep and production was always exciting as well as fun.

Above all, however, it was the characters that captured and beguiled me on that first read; they

are timeless, enchanting, intriguing. All of them are being tested to their core, navigating a world that is becoming ever more complex and dangerous—a world that, however heightened and magical, in some ways echoes our own across time.

David Yates
September 9, 2018

THE
ORIGINAL SCREENPLAY

SCENE 1
EXT. NEW YORK, AMERICAN MINISTRY OF MAGIC—1927—NIGHT

AERIAL SHOT of New York and MACUSA building.

SCENE 2
INT. MACUSA BASEMENT, BARE, BLACK-WALLED ROOM—NIGHT

The long-haired, bearded GRINDELWALD sits motionless, magically fixed to a chair. The air shimmers, charged with spells.

ABERNATHY peers in at GRINDELWALD from the corridor.

A baby Chupacabra—part lizard, part homunculus, a blood-sucking creature of the Americas—is chained to GRINDELWALD'S chair.

SCENE 3
INT. MACUSA, CORRIDOR BETWEEN CELLS— SHORTLY AFTER—NIGHT

PRESIDENT SERAPHINA PICQUERY and RUDOLPH SPIELMAN walk at pace toward an ominous-looking door past endless pairs of guards.

SPIELMAN
(Germanic)
. . . you'll be glad to be rid of
him, I expect.

PICQUERY
We'd be more than happy to
keep him here in custody.

SPIELMAN
Six months are enough. It's

time for him to answer for his crimes in Europe.

As they reach the door, ABERNATHY turns and acknowledges them.

                    ABERNATHY
          President Picquery, Mr.
          Spielman, sir. Prisoner is
          secured and ready to travel.

SPIELMAN and PICQUERY peer into the cell at GRINDELWALD.

                    SPIELMAN
          You've thrown everything at
          him, I see.

                    PICQUERY
          It was necessary. He's
          extremely powerful. We've
          had to change his guard
          three times—he's very . . .
          persuasive. So we removed
          his tongue.

SCENE 4
INT. MACUSA CELLS—NIGHT

Cells resembling cages rise in tiers. Prisoners chant and bang against the bars as the bound GRINDELWALD is transported upstairs, suspended magically in midair.

PRISONERS
Grindelwald! Grindelwald!

SCENE 5
EXT. MACUSA ROOFTOP—MINUTES LATER—NIGHT

A hearse-like black carriage, drawn by eight Thestrals, waits. AURORS 1 & 2 climb into the driver's seat, the rest force GRINDELWALD inside.

SPIELMAN
The wizarding community
worldwide owes you a great
debt, Madam President.

PICQUERY
Do not underestimate him.

ABERNATHY approaches them.

ABERNATHY
Mr. Spielman, we found his
wand hidden away.

He hands over a black rectangular box.

PICQUERY
Abernathy?

ABERNATHY
And we found this.

*He holds a vial of some glowing gold substance in the
palm of his hand. SPIELMAN reaches for the vial, which
hangs on a chain, and after a moment of hesitation,
ABERNATHY releases it.*

*Inside the carriage, GRINDELWALD raises his eyes to the
roof as the vial is passed to SPIELMAN.*

*SPIELMAN climbs into the carriage. AUROR 1 driving,
AUROR 2 beside him. The door closes. A series of padlocks
emerges from the carriage doors. An ominous drumroll of*

clicks as padlocks fasten themselves in place.

> AUROR 1
>
> Yah!

The Thestrals take off.

The carriage plummets, then soars away through torrential rain. More AURORS follow on broomsticks.

A beat.

ABERNATHY steps forward, holding the Elder Wand.
He looks up at the carriage, growing ever smaller.
He Disapparates.

CUT TO:

SCENE 6
EXT. THESTRAL-DRAWN CARRIAGE—NIGHT

The underside of the carriage. ABERNATHY Apparates, clinging to the wheel shaft.

SCENE 7
INT. THESTRAL-DRAWN CARRIAGE—NIGHT

SPIELMAN and GRINDELWALD sit, eyes locked, flanked by AURORS, all pointing their wands at GRINDELWALD. GRINDELWALD'S wand box lies on SPIELMAN'S lap.

SPIELMAN holds up the vial, dangling from its chain.

SPIELMAN

No more silver tongue, eh?

But GRINDELWALD is transforming . . .

SCENE 8
EXT. THESTRAL-DRAWN CARRIAGE—NIGHT

ABERNATHY adjusts his grip underneath the carriage. His face too is changing. His hair is turning blond and

lengthening . . . he is GRINDELWALD. He raises the Elder Wand.

SCENE 9
INT. THESTRAL-DRAWN CARRIAGE—NIGHT

GRINDELWALD'S rapid transformation into a tongueless ABERNATHY is almost complete.

> SPIELMAN
> (*shocked*)

Oh!

SCENE 10
EXT. THESTRAL-DRAWN CARRIAGE—NIGHT

Now fully transformed, GRINDELWALD Disapparates from the underside of the carriage . . .

. . . and Apparates next to the driver's seat, where he is spotted by AURORS 1 & 2. GRINDELWALD points his wand at the carriage reins, turning the black ropes into living snakes that ensnare AUROR 1 so he falls from the carriage, back through the night sky, past the broomstick riders.

GRINDELWALD casts another spell so the black ropes of the reins bind AUROR 2 like a chrysalis, launching him forward in the air, then slingshotting him back to knock AURORS 3 & 4 from the rear of the Thestral-drawn carriage. They fall away into darkness.

SCENE 11
INT. THESTRAL-DRAWN CARRIAGE—NIGHT

All wands reverse their direction to jab dangerously at the necks of SPIELMAN and the two remaining AURORS. SPIELMAN watches as his wand melts into dust.

The carriage rocks dangerously, both doors open. As GRINDELWALD'S head appears at the window, the panicking SPIELMAN opens the wand box on his lap. The Chupacabra leaps out and sinks its fangs deep into SPIELMAN'S neck. He wrestles it. The vial falls to the floor.

SCENE 12
EXT. THESTRAL-DRAWN CARRIAGE—NIGHT

GRINDELWALD drives the carriage down onto the Hudson River, chased by the AURORS on broomsticks. The carriage wheels graze the surface of the water. The broomstick riders are catching up.

GRINDELWALD touches the Elder Wand to the river and at once the inside of the carriage begins to fill with water.

He lifts the carriage back up into the air.

SCENE 13
INT. THESTRAL-DRAWN CARRIAGE—NIGHT

Submerged in the water, the two AURORS, SPIELMAN, and ABERNATHY hold their breath.

SPIELMAN attempts to grab the vial, which is floating

*loose in the water, but the Chupacabra blocks his path.
ABERNATHY, with hands still bound, manages to capture
the vial in his mouth.*

SCENE 14
EXT. THESTRAL-DRAWN CARRIAGE—NIGHT

*Still driving the carriage, GRINDELWALD swirls his
wand in the air toward the surrounding storm clouds.
One by one, forks of lightning strike the broomstick riders,
knocking each in turn from the sky.*

SCENE 15
INT. THESTRAL-DRAWN CARRIAGE—NIGHT

*GRINDELWALD appears at the door and nods to
ABERNATHY. He throws the door open so the water
pours out—along with the two remaining AURORS.
GRINDELWALD clambers inside and retrieves the vial*

from ABERNATHY'S mouth by the chain, casting a spell
that grants ABERNATHY a new forked tongue.

> GRINDELWALD
> You have joined a noble
> cause, my friend.

GRINDELWALD rips the little Chupacabra off
SPIELMAN. It rubs its bloody face affectionately against
his hand.

> GRINDELWALD
> I know. Okay. I know,
> Antonio.

He looks at it with distaste.

> GRINDELWALD
> So needy.

He then flings it through the door.

He blasts SPIELMAN magically through the open door,
then tosses a wand after him.

SCENE 16
EXT. SKY OVER ATLANTIC OCEAN—NIGHT

As SPIELMAN falls, he manages to seize the wand and conjures an invisible Slowing Charm. Sinking slowly toward the sea, SPIELMAN watches his carriage streaking away in the direction of Europe.

SCENE 17
EXT. OVERCAST LONDON, WHITEHALL—
THREE MONTHS LATER—AFTERNOON

A gloomy silence. Establishing shot.

An owl flutters down into the Ministry.

SCENE 18
INT. MINISTRY OF MAGIC—AFTERNOON

NEWT SCAMANDER sits alone in a dingy waiting area, staring abstractedly into space. After a moment, he feels something tugging on his wrist. He looks down. Pickett, a Bowtruckle, is swinging on a loose thread in his cuff.

The thread snaps. Pickett falls. NEWT'S button rolls away down a corridor. NEWT and Pickett watch it go.

A beat.

Then both chase after it. NEWT just gets there first. As he bends to pick it up, he finds himself confronted by a pair of female feet.

LETA (O.S.)
They're ready for you, Newt.

He stands up. Face-to-face with LETA LESTRANGE, who is beautiful and smiling, NEWT stuffs the button and Pickett into his pocket.

NEWT
Leta . . . what are you
doing here?

LETA
Theseus thought it would be
good if I became part of the
Ministry family.

NEWT
Did he actually say the words
"Ministry family"?

She gives a little laugh. They head off along the corridor. Tension. A lot of history.

NEWT
That sounds like my brother.

LETA
Theseus was disappointed you
couldn't come to dinner. Any
of the nights we asked you.

NEWT
Well, I've been busy.

LETA
He's your brother, Newt, he
likes spending time with you.
And so do I.

*NEWT spots Pickett climbing onto his lapel and holds out
the breast pocket of his coat.*

NEWT
(to Pickett)
Oi, you! Hop in, Pick.

Pickett snuggles down.

LETA
(smiling)
Why do strange creatures

love you so much?

NEWT
Well, there are no
strange creatures—

NEWT & LETA
"—only blinkered people."

She is smiling again. NEWT—just—reciprocates.

LETA
How long did you get in
detention for saying that
to Prendergast?

NEWT
You know, I think it was a
month that time.

LETA
And I set off a Dungbomb
under his desk so I could join
you, do you remember?

*They have come within sight of scary, official doors leading
to the meeting room. THESEUS SCAMANDER emerges.*

NEWT

No, I actually don't
remember that.

*Rebuffed, she comes to a halt. NEWT walks away toward
THESEUS, who is very like NEWT, but more outgoing,
easier in manner. THESEUS winks at LETA before
turning to NEWT.*

THESEUS

Hello.

LETA

Theseus. We were just
talking about Newt coming
for dinner.

THESEUS

Really? Well . . . Look, before
we go in there I—

NEWT

—It's my fifth attempt,
Theseus. I know the form.

THESEUS

This isn't going to be like
the other times. This is . . .

Just try and keep an open
mind, will you? And maybe a
little less—

*A wordless gesture indicates Pickett, NEWT'S blue coat,
and his messy hair.*

NEWT

—like me?

THESEUS
(not without affection)
Well, it can't hurt. Come on,
let's go.

SCENE 19
INT. MINISTRY OF MAGIC, HEARING ROOM—
AFTERNOON

*NEWT and THESEUS enter the room, where TORQUIL
TRAVERS (harsh, mean-spirited), ARNOLD GUZMAN
(American), and RUDOLPH SPIELMAN (who is still
bruised from GRINDELWALD'S escape, the bloody bite
visible on his neck) are already sitting.*

Two empty chairs, which NEWT and THESEUS take. The corners of the room are in darkness.

> TRAVERS
> Hearing commences.

The quill begins to write. TRAVERS opens a file in front of him, which contains pictures of NEWT'S Wanted pictures and of the post-Obscurial devastation in New York.

> TRAVERS
> You want an end to the
> ban on your traveling
> internationally. Why?

> NEWT
> Because I like to travel
> internationally.

> SPIELMAN
> (*reading from his own file*)
> "Subject uncooperative and
> evasive on reasons for last
> international trip."

All look at NEWT, waiting.

NEWT
It was a field trip. I was
collecting material for my
book on magical beasts—

TRAVERS
You destroyed half of
New York.

NEWT
No, that's actually factually
incorrect on two counts—

THESEUS
(*quiet but stern*)
Newt!

NEWT stops, frowns.

GUZMAN
Mr. Scamander, it's clear
you're frustrated and, frankly,
so are we. In the spirit of
compromise, we'd like to
make a proposition.

NEWT glances at THESEUS warily. THESEUS nods: Listen.

NEWT
What kind of proposition?

TRAVERS
The committee will agree
to lift your travel ban under
one condition.

NEWT waits. SPIELMAN leans forward.

SPIELMAN
You join the Ministry.
Specifically, your
brother's department.

NEWT digests this, then:

NEWT
No, I—that isn't my kind of—
Theseus is the Auror. I think
my talents lie elsewhere—

GUZMAN
Mr. Scamander. The wizarding
and non-wizarding worlds
have been at peace for over a
century. Grindelwald wants to
see that peace destroyed, and

for certain members of our
community his message is very
seductive. Many purebloods
believe it is their birthright to
rule not only our world but the
non-magic world as well. They
see Grindelwald as their hero,
and Grindelwald sees this boy
as a means to make this all
come true.

*Hearing this, NEWT frowns, watching as CREDENCE'S
face emerges in the surface of the table.*

NEWT
I'm sorry. You're talking
about Credence as if he were
still here.

THESEUS
He survived, Newt.

*NEWT stops cold, his eyes fixed on THESEUS.
THESEUS nods.*

THESEUS
He's still alive. He left New
York months ago. He's

somewhere in Europe. Where
exactly, we don't know, but—

NEWT
And you want me to hunt
Credence down? To kill him?

*Out of the shadows in the corner comes deep, nasty
laughter.*

GRIMMSON
Same old Scamander.

*NEWT reacts to the sound of the voice. GRIMMSON
moves into the light. Scarred, brutal, he is a beast hunter
for hire.*

NEWT
(*furious*)
What's he doing here?

GRIMMSON
Taking on the job you're too
soft to do.

*GRIMMSON walks toward them while the ghostly image
of CREDENCE shimmers on the enchanted surface of
the table.*

GRIMMSON
(of CREDENCE)
Is that it?

NEWT rises furiously, storms toward the door.

TRAVERS
(calling after him)
Travel documentation
denied!

*THESEUS stares at the door as it closes. The
committee looks unsurprised, turns their gazes to the
smirking GRIMMSON.*

SCENE 20
**INT. MINISTRY OF MAGIC, CORRIDOR—
AFTERNOON**

THESEUS chases after NEWT.

THESEUS
Newt!

NEWT stops. Turns.

>   THESEUS
>   *(testy)*
>   You think I like the idea of
>   Grimmson any more than
>   you do?
>
>   NEWT
>   Listen, I don't want to hear
>   how the ends justify the
>   means, Theseus.
>
>   THESEUS
>   I think you're gonna have
>   to pull your head out of
>   the sand!
>
>   NEWT
>   *(exasperated)*
>   Okay, right, here we go. What
>   a selfish . . . irresponsible . . .
>
>   THESEUS
>   You know, the time is coming
>   when everyone's going to
>   have to pick a side. Even you.

NEWT
I don't do sides.

THESEUS
Newt . . .

He turns to go, but THESEUS runs after him, grabs his arm to hold him back.

THESEUS
(pulling him in for a hug)
C'mere.

NEWT doesn't reciprocate but doesn't fight him off either.

THESEUS
(in NEWT'S ear)
They're watching you.

SCENE 21
INT. MINISTRY OF MAGIC, HEARING ROOM—
AFTERNOON

*GRIMMSON is sitting in what was NEWT'S seat, facing
the committee.*

> GRIMMSON
> Well, gentlemen. I assume
> this means I have the job.

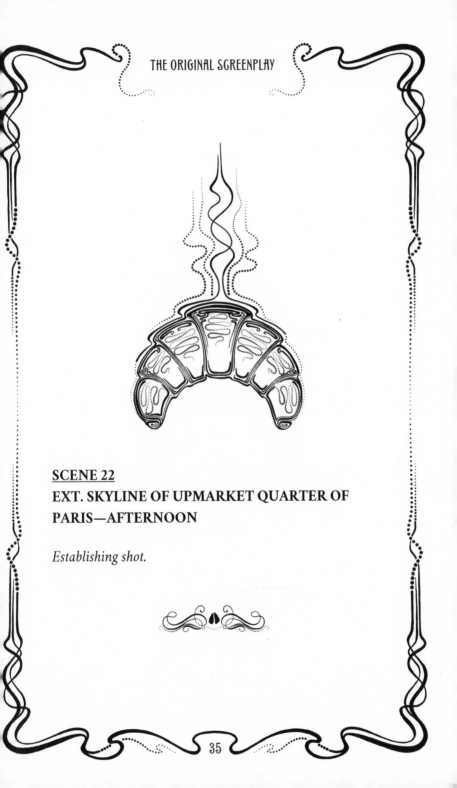

SCENE 22
EXT. SKYLINE OF UPMARKET QUARTER OF PARIS—AFTERNOON

Establishing shot.

SCENE 23
EXT. ELEGANT STREET OF 19TH CENTURY
PARISIAN HOUSES—AFTERNOON

GRINDELWALD and ACOLYTES stand in the street.
GRINDELWALD points his cane at a particularly fine
house.

A clatter announces the arrival of a horse-drawn hearse.

NAGEL, KRALL, CARROW, ABERNATHY,
KRAFFT, ROSIER (female), and MACDUFF approach
the front door. KRALL opens it with his wand. The
ACOLYTES enter.

> PARISIAN MAN (O.S.)
> Chérie?

> PARISIAN WOMAN (O.S.)
> (worried)
> Qui est là?

GRINDELWALD looks around the street, calm, waiting,
tapping on the pavement with his cane.

We see a green flash—the Killing Curse. The door reopens.
Two black coffins exit. GRINDELWALD watches as
NAGEL and KRAFFT load the coffins onto the carriage.

SCENE 24
INT. GRINDELWALD'S HIDEOUT, DRAWING ROOM— AFTERNOON

GRINDELWALD surveys the elegant clutter left by the haut bourgeois family he has just murdered.

> GRINDELWALD
> Yes. This will be suitable after
> a thorough cleanse.
> *(to NAGEL)*
> I want you to go to the
> circus now. Give my note to
> Credence, begin his journey.

NAGEL nods and leaves.

> ROSIER
> When we've won, they'll flee
> cities in the millions. They've
> had their time.

> GRINDELWALD
> We don't say such things out
> loud. We want only freedom.

Freedom to be ourselves.

ROSIER
To annihilate non-wizards.

GRINDELWALD
Not all of them. Not all. We're
not merciless. The beast of
burden will always be necessary.

We hear the sound of a child close at hand.

SCENE 25
INT. GRINDELWALD'S HIDEOUT, NURSERY—
AFTERNOON

GRINDELWALD enters. A small child looks up, puzzled.
GRINDELWALD contemplates him for a moment, then
nods at CARROW and turns to leave.

We see another green flash as GRINDELWALD closes
the door.

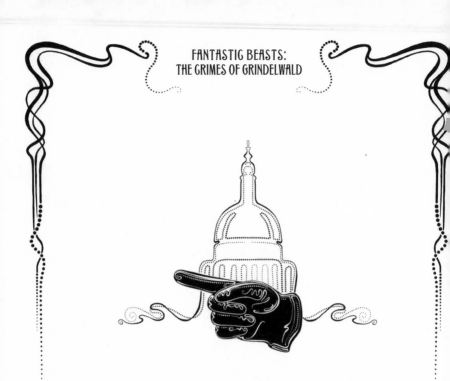

SCENE 26
EXT. LONDON BACK STREET—EVENING

*NEWT Apparates and walks on briskly beneath an
increasingly stormy sky. Seconds later, STEBBINS, an
Auror, Apparates some yards behind him. They have been
playing this game for an hour. NEWT turns a corner into a
darker alleyway, peers back around the corner, and points
his wand back at STEBBINS.*

> NEWT
> (sotto voce)
>
> *Ventus.*

STEBBINS is immediately caught in a hurricane for one. To the confusion and amusement of passing Muggles, his hat flies away, he is almost knocked off his feet, and cannot proceed.

Smiling slightly, NEWT withdraws his head, still leaning against the wall of the dark alleyway, to find a single black glove hanging in the air in front of him. He looks at it, expressionless. It gives a little wave, then points into the far distance. NEWT looks to where it is pointing. High on the dome of St. Paul's Cathedral, a tiny human figure raises its arm.

NEWT looks back at the glove, which makes as though to shake hands. NEWT takes it, and he and the glove Disapparate—

SCENE 27
EXT. DOME OF ST. PAUL'S—EVENING

—Apparating beside a dandyesque forty-five-year-old wizard with graying auburn hair and beard. NEWT hands back his glove.

NEWT
Dumbledore.
(amused)
Were the less conspicuous
rooftops full, then?

DUMBLEDORE
(looking out over city)
I do enjoy a view. *Nebulus.*

A swirling fog descends over London.

They Disapparate.

SCENE 28
EXT. TRAFALGAR SQUARE—EVENING

*DUMBLEDORE and NEWT Apparate and walk on
past the great stone Landseer lions. The darkening sky is
becoming increasingly ominous. A flock of pigeons rises
into the air at their approach.*

DUMBLEDORE
How was it?

NEWT

They're still convinced that
you sent me to New York.

DUMBLEDORE

You told them I didn't?

NEWT

Yes. Even though you did.

A beat. DUMBLEDORE inscrutable, NEWT
wanting answers.

NEWT

You told me where to find
that trafficked Thunderbird,
Dumbledore. You knew that
I would take him home and
you knew I'd have to take
him through a Muggle port.

DUMBLEDORE

Well, I've always felt an
affinity with the great magical
birds. There's a story in my
family that a phoenix will
come to any Dumbledore
who is in desperate need.

They say my great-great-
grandfather had one, but that
it took flight when he died,
never to return.

NEWT
With all due respect, I don't
believe for a minute that's
why you told me about
the Thunderbird.

*A noise behind them. The silhouette of a man appears out
of shadows. They Disapparate—*

SCENE 29
EXT. VICTORIA BUS STATION—EVENING

*Footsteps nearby. Both ready their wands, but the footsteps
die away. They walk on.*

DUMBLEDORE
Credence is in Paris, Newt.
He's trying to trace his real

family. I take it you've heard
the rumors about who he
really is?

NEWT

No.

DUMBLEDORE and NEWT board a stationary bus.

DUMBLEDORE
The purebloods think he's the
last of an important French
line, a baby whom everyone
thought lost . . .

A look between them. NEWT is astonished.

NEWT
Not Leta's brother?

DUMBLEDORE
That's what they're
whispering. Pureblood or
not, I know this: An Obscurus
grows in the absence of love
as a dark twin, an only friend.
If Credence has a real brother
or sister out there who can

take its place, he might yet
be saved.
            (*beat*)
Wherever Credence is in
Paris, he's either in danger or
a danger to others. We may
not know who he is yet, but
he needs to be found. And I
rather hoped you might be
the one to find him.

*DUMBLEDORE conjures NICOLAS FLAMEL'S
card from thin air and offers it to NEWT, who eyes it
with suspicion.*

NEWT
What's that?

DUMBLEDORE
It's an address of a very old
acquaintance of mine. A safe
house in Paris, reinforced
with enchantments.

NEWT
Safe house? Why would I
need a safe house in Paris?

DUMBLEDORE
One hopes you won't, but
should things at some point
go terribly wrong, it's good to
have a place to go. You know,
for a cup of tea.

NEWT
No, no, no—absolutely not.

SCENE 30
EXT. LAMBETH BRIDGE—NIGHT

They Apparate onto a bridge.

NEWT
I'm banned from
international travel,
Dumbledore. If I leave the
country, they will put me in
Azkaban and throw away
the key.

DUMBLEDORE stops.

> DUMBLEDORE
> Do you know why I admire
> you, Newt? More, perhaps,
> than any man I know?
> *(off NEWT'S surprise)*
> You don't seek power or
> popularity. You simply ask,
> is the thing right in itself?
> If it is, then I must do it, no
> matter the cost.

He walks on.

> NEWT
> That's all very well,
> Dumbledore, but, forgive me
> for asking, why can't you go?

They stop.

> DUMBLEDORE
> I can't move against
> Grindelwald. It has to be you.
> *(beat)*
> Well, I don't blame you,
> in your shoes I'd probably

refuse too. It's late. Good
evening, Newt.

DUMBLEDORE Disapparates.

> NEWT

Oh c'mon!

*DUMBLEDORE'S empty glove reappears and tucks the
business card bearing the address of the safe house into
NEWT'S top pocket.*

> NEWT
> *(exasperated)*

Dumbledore.

<u>SCENE 31</u>
EXT. NEWT'S STREET—NIGHT

*Establishing shot: a street of ordinary yellow brick
Victorian houses. First specks of rain. NEWT walks swiftly
up the front steps but pauses just outside the front door.
The light in his sitting room is flashing on and off.*

SCENE 32
INT. NEWT'S HOUSE—NIGHT

NEWT opens the front door cautiously. Inside, a baby Niffler is swinging from the brass cord of a table lamp, causing the light to flicker on and off. The baby Niffler succeeds in stealing the brass cord before spotting NEWT. It scampers away, knocking all manner of objects to the floor.

NEWT spots a second baby Niffler sitting on a set of weighing scales, pinned down by gold-colored weights it is clearly attempting to steal.

As the first baby makes it to the dining table, NEWT lightly drops a saucepan on top of it, which continues moving across the table. NEWT tosses an apple into the opposite weighing scale, sending the baby Niffler flying into the air. NEWT catches both baby Nifflers as they fall, then tucks them into his pockets.

Satisfied, NEWT heads toward the door to his basement but turns at the last moment to see a third escaped baby Niffler climbing onto a bottle of champagne on the counter. With a sense of inevitability, the champagne bottle pops and the baby Niffler zooms toward NEWT on top of the cork, soaring past him and down the stairs to the basement.

SCENE 33
INT. NEWT'S BASEMENT MENAGERIE—
MOMENTS LATER—NIGHT

A gigantic hospital for magical creatures.

NEWT
Bunty! Bunty! Bunty, the
baby Nifflers are loose again!
(to the Nifflers)
Oi! Oh.

*BUNTY, NEWT'S assistant, hurries into view. She is a plain
girl, crazy about creatures, hopelessly in love with NEWT.
She peels off the Nifflers with freshly bandaged fingers.*

*She tempts the last baby Niffler—the champagne cork
rider—with a gold necklace, then tucks all three into a nest
full of sparkling objects.*

NEWT

Well done.

BUNTY

I'm so sorry, Newt, they
must have picked the lock
while I was cleaning out
the Augureys—

NEWT

Not to worry.

NEWT and BUNTY walk together among the enclosures.

BUNTY

Hmm . . . I've fed nearly
everyone, Pinky's had his
nose drops, and—

NEWT

—And Elsie?

BUNTY

Elsie's droppings are nearly
normal again.

NEWT

Wonderful. You can clock

off now—
　　　　(seeing her fingers)
I told you to leave the Kelpie
to me.

BUNTY
That wound needs
more ointment—

NEWT
I don't want you losing
fingers over it.

*NEWT marches toward a patch of black water, BUNTY
trotting in his wake, awash with emotion at his concern
for her.*

NEWT
Seriously, you go home
now, Bunty. You must
be exhausted.

BUNTY
You know the Kelpie's easier
with two.

*They approach the water. NEWT unhooks a bridle hanging
beside the pond.*

BUNTY
(*hopeful*)
Perhaps you should take off
your shirt?

NEWT
(*oblivious*)
Don't worry, I'll dry off
quickly enough.

NEWT smiles and jumps backward into the water. The Kelpie erupts: a gigantic, semi-spectral horse intent on drowning NEWT, who grabs it around the neck and manages to scramble onto its back as it thrashes.

The Kelpie dives, taking NEWT with it. BUNTY waits, frightened.

WHOOSH—NEWT bursts back out of the water and the Kelpie is bridled. Now docile, it shakes its mane. BUNTY transfixed by the sight of NEWT in his wet shirt.

NEWT
Someone needed to let off
some steam. Ointment, Bunty?

She hands it over. Still mounted, NEWT applies ointment to a wound on the Kelpie's neck.

NEWT

Bite Bunty again and there'll
be trouble, mister.

As he dismounts, there is a crash from overhead. Both he and BUNTY look up.

BUNTY
(scared)

What was that?

NEWT

I don't know. But I want you
to go home now, Bunty.

BUNTY

Shall I call the Ministry?

NEWT

No, I want you to go home.
Please.

SCENE 34
INT. NEWT'S STAIRCASE—A MINUTE LATER—NIGHT

NEWT climbs the stairs to his living quarters, wand drawn, curious and expecting the worst. He pushes open the door.

SCENE 35
INT. NEWT'S SITTING ROOM—NIGHT

A spartan bachelor residence. NEWT'S real life is in the basement.

JACOB KOWALSKI and QUEENIE GOLDSTEIN stand in the middle of the room, suitcases beside them, QUEENIE nervous and excited, JACOB unfocused and over-merry, possibly drunk. He is holding the remaining pieces of NEWT'S vase, which he has just broken.

> QUEENIE
> If you could just give it to
> me . . . Just give it to me,

sweetie. Just give it to me.
(whispering)
If you could just give this to
me, sweetheart. Oh!

JACOB
(looking at NEWT)
He doesn't care. Hold it.

NEWT

St—

JACOB
(bellows)
HEY! NEWT! Get over here,
you maniac.

He flings his arms around a delighted but awkward NEWT.

QUEENIE
We hope you don't mind,
Newt? We let ourselves in—
it's raining out there—cats
and dogs! London's cold!

NEWT
(to JACOB)
But you were supposed to

have been Obliviated!

JACOB

I know!

NEWT

So . . . But . . .

JACOB

It didn't work, pal. I mean,
you said it, the potion only
erases bad memories. I didn't
have any. I mean, don't get
me wrong, I had some weird
ones. But this angel . . . this
angel over here, she filled me
in on all the bad parts, and
here we are, I guess, huh?

NEWT
(overjoyed)
This is wonderful!

He looks around, sure that TINA is here too.

NEWT
Is . . . Tina? Tina?

QUEENIE
Oh it's just us, honey. Me
and Jacob.

NEWT
Oh.

QUEENIE
(*uncomfortable*)
Why don't I make us some
dinner, huh?

JACOB
Yes!

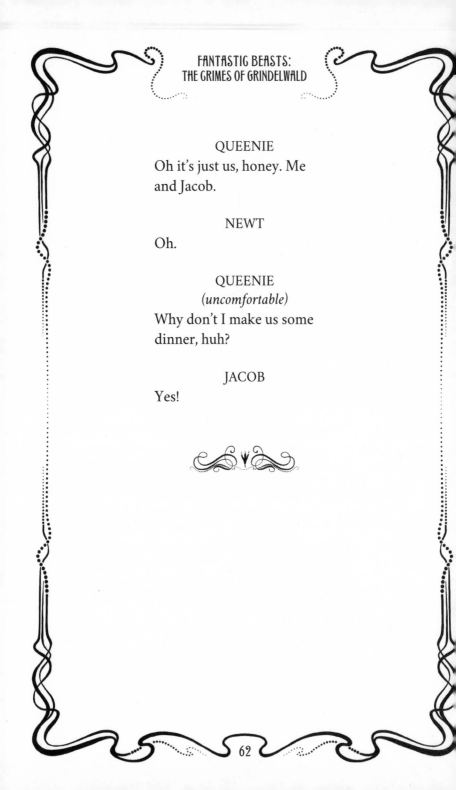

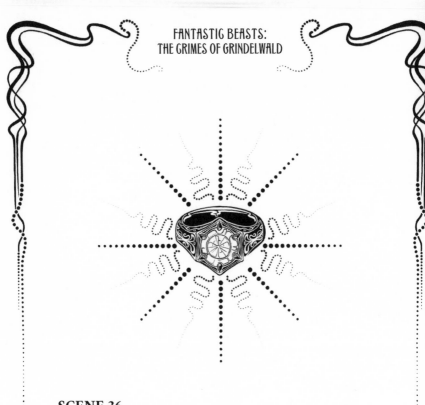

SCENE 36
INT. NEWT'S SITTING ROOM—FIVE MINUTES LATER—NIGHT

The threesome sit at a table bearing NEWT'S mismatched crockery, the atmosphere tainted by TINA'S absence. QUEENIE'S case lies open on the sofa.

> QUEENIE
> Tina and I aren't talking.

> NEWT

Why?

JACOB'S POV—pink and hazy, as though happily drunk.

> QUEENIE
>
> Oh well, you know, she found
> out about Jacob and I seeing
> each other and she didn't like
> it, 'cause of the "law."
> *(miming quotation marks)*
> Not allowed to date No-Majs,
> not allowed to marry them.
> Blah, blah, blah. Well, she was
> all in a tizzy anyway, 'cause
> of you.

> NEWT
>
> Me?

> QUEENIE
>
> Yeah, you, Newt. It was in
> *Spellbound*. Here—I brought it
> for you—

She points her wand at her suitcase. A celebrity magazine zooms to her: Spellbound: Celebrity Secrets and Spell Tips of the Stars! *On the cover, an idealized NEWT and an improbably beaming Niffler.* BEAST TAMER NEWT TO WED!

QUEENIE opens the magazine. THESEUS, LETA,

NEWT, and BUNTY stand side by side at his book launch.

> QUEENIE
> *(showing him)*
> "Newt Scamander with
> fiancée, Leta Lestrange;
> brother, Theseus; and
> unknown woman."

> NEWT
> No. Theseus is marrying Leta,
> not me.

> QUEENIE
> Oh! Oh dear . . . well, see,
> Teen read that, and she
> started dating someone else.
> He's an Auror. His name's
> Achilles Tolliver.

*A silence. Then NEWT starts to notice JACOB'S state:
Eating sloppily, he hums to himself, then tries to drink the
salt. QUEENIE takes it and puts his glass in his hand,
trying to cover.*

> QUEENIE
> Anyway . . . We're real excited
> to be here, Newt. This is

a—well, it's a special trip for
us. You see, Jacob and I, we're
getting married.

*She shows him her engagement ring. JACOB tries to toast
the moment and pours beer all over his ear.*

JACOB
I'm marrying Jacob!

*Now sure he knows what's going on, NEWT glares
at QUEENIE.*

NEWT (V.O.)
(speaking telepathically)
You've enchanted him,
haven't you?

QUEENIE
(reading his mind)
What? I have not.

NEWT
Will you stop reading my
mind?
(speaking telepathically)
Queenie, you've brought him
here against his will.

QUEENIE
Oh, that is an outrageous
accusation. Look at him. He's
just happy. He's so happy!

NEWT
(*drawing his wand*)
Then you won't mind if I—

QUEENIE jumps up and tries to shield JACOB from him.

QUEENIE
Please don't!

NEWT
Queenie, you've got nothing
to fear if he wants to get
married. We can just lift the
enchantment and he can tell
us himself.

Several painful moments pass. At last she moves aside.

JACOB
What you got there? Whatchu
gonna do? Whatchu gonna do
with that, Mr. Scamander?

NEWT

Surgito.

JACOB reacts as though to a bucket of cold water. He comes back to himself and takes in his surroundings. He looks at NEWT.

NEWT
Congratulations on your
engagement, Jacob.

JACOB
Wait, what?

NEWT looks at QUEENIE.

JACOB
Oh no.

He realizes he has been taken against his will. Slowly, he gets to his feet to face QUEENIE.

She reads his mind. With a sob, she runs to close her case (several small objects, including a lipstick and a fragment of torn postcard, fall out) and flees the apartment.

JACOB
Queenie!

(*turning to NEWT*)
It's very nice to see you.
Where the hell am I
right now?

NEWT
Uh, uh, London.

JACOB
(*frustrated*)
Oh! I always wanted to
go here!
(*angry*)
Queenie!

He runs after her.

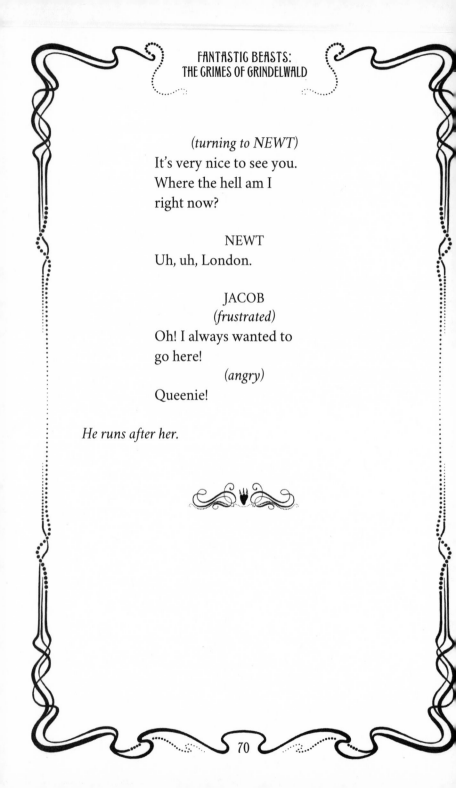

SCENE 37
EXT. NEWT'S STREET—A MINUTE LATER—NIGHT

QUEENIE dashes out of NEWT'S house and off up the street, crying. JACOB runs after her, livid.

> JACOB
> Queen, honey. Well, I'm
> just curious, when were you
> going to wake me up? After
> we'd had five kids?

QUEENIE turns to confront JACOB.

> QUEENIE
> Why is it wrong to want to
> marry you?

> JACOB
> Okay—

> QUEENIE
> To wanna have a family? I
> just want what everyone else
> has, that's all.

JACOB

Okay, wait. We talked about
this, like, a million times. If
we get married and they find
out, they're gonna throw you
in jail, sweetheart. I can't have
that. They don't like people
like me marrying people
like you. I ain't a wizard. I'm
just me.

QUEENIE

They're really progressive
here, and they'll let us get
married properly.

QUEENIE gestures to the street.

JACOB

Sweetheart, you don't need
to enchant me. I'm already
enchanted! I love you
so much.

QUEENIE

Yeah?

JACOB
Yeah. But I can't have you
risking everything like this,
you know? You're not giving
us a choice, sweetheart.

QUEENIE
You're not givin' *me* a choice.
One of us had to be brave,
and you were being a coward!

JACOB
I was being a coward? If I'm a
coward, you're a—

She reads his mind.

QUEENIE
—crazy!

She reacts. He knows she "heard" him.

JACOB
I didn't say it . . .

QUEENIE
You didn't have to.

JACOB
No, I didn't mean it,
sweetheart.

QUEENIE
Yeah, you did.

JACOB
No.

QUEENIE
I'm gonna go see my sister.

JACOB
Fine. See your sister.

QUEENIE
Fine.

QUEENIE Disapparates.

JACOB
No, wait! No! Queenie!
I didn't mean it. I didn't
say nothing.

But he is alone in the street.

SCENE 38
INT. NEWT'S HOUSE—SHORTLY AFTER—
NIGHT

NEWT'S miserable gaze falls on the piece of postcard. He crosses to pick it up, then points his wand at it.

NEWT

Papyrus Reparo.

It reconstitutes into a whole. We see a picture of Paris.

Postcard text becomes visible onscreen.

TINA (V.O.)

My dear Queenie,
What a beautiful city.
I'm thinking of you,
Tina X

SCENE 39
INT. NEWT'S BASEMENT MENAGERIE—NIGHT

CLOSE ON JACOB as he enters, pushes open the door, stares around. Soaked through, he has been searching the streets for an hour. NEWT is nowhere to be seen.

JACOB

Hey, Newt?

NEWT (O.S.)

Down here, Jacob. I'll be with
you in a second.

JACOB starts peering into the enclosure. By the patch of

*dark water where the Kelpie lives, NEWT has placed a
sign for BUNTY:* BUNTY, DON'T TOUCH UNTIL I GET BACK.
He walks on.

An Augurey caws mournfully at JACOB as he walks past.

JACOB
I got my own problems.

NEWT (O.S.)
No, no, no. Back in, please.
Right, wait, wait, wait, wait.

A sign on the Augurey cage reads: BUNTY—DON'T FORGET TO
GIVE PATRICK PELLETS. *JACOB hears movement and changes
direction, passing a snoozing griffin with a bandaged beak:*
BUNTY: CHANGE DRESSING DAILY.

*NEWT'S case sits beside the Niffler enclosure. On the
inside of the lid is a large moving picture of TINA he has
torn out of a newspaper.*

NEWT comes round the corner wearing his coat.

NEWT
Queenie left a postcard.
Tina's in Paris looking
for Credence.

JACOB

Genius. Queenie's gonna go
straight for Tina.
(*elated*)
Okay, we're going to France,
pal! Hold on. I'll get my jacket.

NEWT

I've got it.

*NEWT has already pointed his wand at the ceiling.
JACOB'S coat, hat, and case drop onto the floor in front of
him. JACOB is blasted with warm magical air, which dries
his rain-soaked clothes.*

JACOB
(*impressed*)
Oh. Beautiful.

They leave. We close in on the note that has appeared:
BUNTY, GONE TO PARIS. HAVE TAKEN NIFFLERS WITH ME. NEWT.

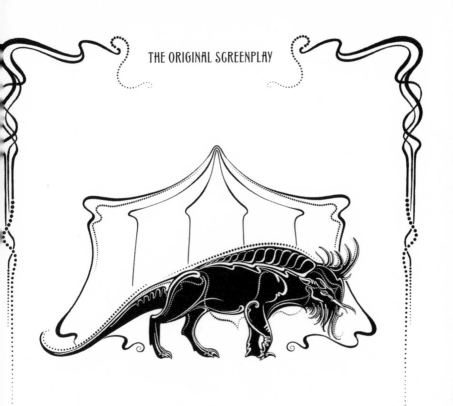

SCENE 40
EXT. PARIS, PLACE CACHÉE—NIGHT

A clear, starry night. TINA GOLDSTEIN, reinstated Auror on a mission of her own, more elegant and confident than in New York but carrying private sadness, walks toward the bronzed statue of a robed woman set on a tall stone base, where witches and wizards dressed as Muggles are vanishing.

SCENE 41
EXT. PLACE CACHÉE, CIRCUS ARCANUS—
NIGHT

Music, laughter, and conversation erupt around her. The circus is now in full swing. A banner declares: CIRCUS ARCANUS: FREAKS AND ODDITIES! *Several tents, a big top in the middle.*

TINA walks past the street performers working in the open, scrutinizing them. A HALF-TROLL performs feats of strength. A few misshapen and particularly downtrodden humanoids—UNDERBEINGS without powers but of magical ancestry—shuffle around, taking money from the crowd. Horns hidden beneath hats, unusual eyes beneath hoods; HALF-ELVES and HALF-GOBLINS juggle and tumble.

A magnificent Chinese Zouwu, a giant catlike creature with a long, plumed tail, is imprisoned in a cage. Fireworks burst overhead.

SCENE 42
INT. CIRCUS ARCANUS, FREAKS' TENT—
EVENING

NAGINI is kneeling at a trunk, stroking her circus dress. She must perform shortly. CREDENCE hurries to her.

> CREDENCE
> (*whispers*)
>
> Nagini!

She turns.

> NAGINI
>
> Credence.

He hands her the note. She scans it, frowns.

> CREDENCE
> (*whispers*)
> I think I know where she is.

NAGINI looks up, meets his eyes.

> CREDENCE
> We escape tonight.

SKENDER comes into NAGINI'S tent.

SKENDER

Hey, I've told you to stay
away from her, boy—did I say
you could take a break? Clean
out the Kappa.

*SKENDER closes the curtain between CREDENCE
and NAGINI.*

SKENDER
(*to NAGINI*)
And you, get ready!

*CREDENCE turns and looks up to a cage full
of Firedrakes.*

<u>SCENE 43</u>
INT. CIRCUS ARCANUS, BIG TOP—NIGHT

SKENDER is standing beside the circular platform/cage in the middle of a crowd, many of whom are drunk.

SKENDER

Next in our little show of
freaks and oddities, I present
to you—a Maledictus!

He whips open the curtains. There stands NAGINI in a snakeskin dress. Men in the crowd whistle and jeer.

SKENDER

Once trapped in the jungles of
Indonesia, she is the carrier of a
blood curse. Such Underbeings
are destined, through the
course of their lives, to turn
permanently into beasts.

TINA makes her way around the back of the crowd,
looking for CREDENCE.

Elsewhere in the tent, an elegant, suited French African,
YUSUF KAMA, is scanning the crowd rather than
watching SKENDER. There is a black feather in the band
of his fedora.

SKENDER

But look at her. So beautiful,
yes? So desirable . . . but soon
she will be trapped forever in a
very different body. Every night,
when she sleeps . . . mesdames
et messieurs . . . she is forced
to become—

Nothing happens. The crowd jeers at SKENDER. NAGINI
looks at SKENDER, a look of hatred.

> SKENDER
> She is forced to become . . .

CREDENCE'S and NAGINI'S eyes meet across the big top.

ANGLE ON TINA, who has spotted CREDENCE. She starts to edge toward him, trying not to attract attention.

ANGLE ON KAMA, who does the same.

> SKENDER
> She is forced to become . . .

SKENDER whips the bars. NAGINI closes her eyes. Slowly, she melts into coils.

> SKENDER
> Over time, she will not be
> able to transform back. She
> will be forever trapped in the
> body of a snake.

NAGINI suddenly strikes at SKENDER through the bars and utters a cry in Parseltongue. SKENDER crumples, bleeding. At the back of the tent, CREDENCE smashes open the Firedrakes' cage and they soar to freedom like fireworks. The big top catches fire—screams, panic, the crowd falls over one another to reach the exit—

SCENE 44
EXT. CIRCUS ARCANUS, BIG TOP—NIGHT

The big top is on fire. Firedrakes weave patterns in the sky above it, trailing showers of sparks. The fire has terrified and enraged the creatures. A hippogriff is rearing and plunging while its handlers try to control it. Everywhere performers are packing up, fast, elves shutting themselves into boxes, which fold smaller and smaller.

TINA Apparates and, with a flick of her wand, puts out the fire.

The Zouwu crate is on fire and shaking perilously. The creature within roars and howls. The Zouwu explodes out of it: a monstrous cat the size of an elephant, five-colored, with a tail as long as a python. It has been horrendously abused: Scars across its face, it is malnourished, limping, and now driven to a frenzy of terror.

TINA spots CREDENCE in the distance.

TINA

Credence!

The Zouwu hobbles as fast as it can, away into the darkness. SKENDER knows there is no catching it now. He runs to galvanize his workers.

SKENDER

Pack it up! Paris is done for
us now.

SKENDER points his wand at the tent, shrinks it to the size of a handkerchief, and pockets it.

TINA
(approaching SKENDER)
The boy with the Maledictus,
what do you know about
him?

SKENDER
(contemptuous)
He's looking for his mother.

All my freaks think they can
go home. Okay, let's go.

*He leaps up onto a carriage and, as the crates and boxes
are all magically reduced to a few cases, clatters away into
the night.*

*TINA is left on her own in what seems for a moment to be
a deserted square. Then she realizes that KAMA is standing
behind her.*

CUT TO:

SCENE 45
EXT. PARISIAN CAFÉ—NIGHT

*TINA and KAMA sit together at an outside table. TINA is
suspicious of KAMA.*

> TINA
> I think we were both at the
> circus for the same reason,
> monsieur . . . ?

KAMA

Kama. Yusuf Kama. And you
think right.

TINA

What do you want with Credence?

KAMA

The same as you.

TINA

Which is?

KAMA

To prove who the boy
really is. If the rumors of his
identity are correct, he and I
are—distantly—related. I am
the last male of my pure-
blooded line . . . and so, if the
rumors are correct, is he.

KAMA takes The Predictions of Tycho Dodonus *out of
his pocket and holds it tantalizingly before her.*

KAMA

You have read *The Predictions
of Tycho Dodonus?*

TINA

Yes. But that's poetry,
not proof.

KAMA

If I could show you
something better—more
concrete—something that
proves who he is—would
the Ministries of Europe and
America let him live?

A beat.

TINA

They might.

KAMA
(he nods)
Then come.

He gets up and TINA follows.

SCENE 46
INT. GRINDELWALD'S HIDEOUT, DRAWING ROOM—NIGHT

GRINDELWALD exhales vapor from a glowing skull-shaped hookah. His ACOLYTES watch as the smoke forms a vision of the Obscurus, a swirl of black and flashing red, then resolves into an image of CREDENCE.

All look excited, except KRALL, who is sulky.

> GRINDELWALD
> So . . . Credence Barebone.
> Nearly destroyed by the
> woman who raised him. Yet
> now he seeks the mother
> who bore him. He's desperate
> for family. He's desperate
> for love. He's the key to
> our victory.

> KRALL
> Well, we know where the boy
> is, don't we? Why don't we
> grab him and leave!

GRINDELWALD
(to KRALL)
He must come to me freely—
and he will.

GRINDELWALD returns his gaze to the vision of
CREDENCE suspended in the center of the drawing room.

GRINDELWALD
The path has been laid, and
he is following it. The trail
that will lead him to me, and
the strange and glorious truth
of who he is.

KRALL
Why is he so important?

GRINDELWALD walks to face KRALL.

GRINDELWALD
Who represents the greatest
threat to our cause?

KRALL
Albus Dumbledore.

GRINDELWALD
If I asked you now to go to
the school where he is hiding
and kill him for me, would
you do it for me, Krall?
(*smiles*)
Credence is the only entity
alive . . . who can kill him.

KRALL
You really think that he
can kill the great—can kill
Albus Dumbledore?

GRINDELWALD
(*whispers*)
I know he can. But will
you be with us when that
happens, Krall? Will you?

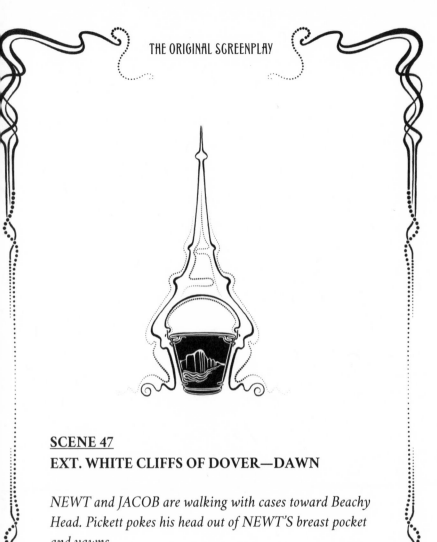

SCENE 47
EXT. WHITE CLIFFS OF DOVER—DAWN

NEWT and JACOB are walking with cases toward Beachy Head. Pickett pokes his head out of NEWT'S breast pocket and yawns.

> NEWT
> Jacob, that man Tina's
> been seeing—

JACOB
Don't worry! She's gonna see
you and she'll see the four of
us together, it'll be just like
New York all over again.
Don't worry about it.

NEWT
Yes, but he's an Auror,
Queenie said?

JACOB
Yeah, he's an Auror. So what?
Don't worry about him.

A beat. They walk.

NEWT
What d'you think I should say
to her, if I see her?

JACOB
Oh, well, it's best not to plan
these things. You know, you
just say whatever comes to
you in the moment.

A beat. They walk.

NEWT
(*reminiscently*)
She has eyes just like
a salamander.

JACOB
Don't say that.

A beat. JACOB decides NEWT needs help.

JACOB
Nah, look, you just tell her
that you missed her. Right,
and then you came all the
way to Paris to find her. She'll
love that. And then, tell her
you're losing sleep at night
for thinking of her. Just
don't say anything about no
salamanders, all right?

NEWT
Right. Okay.

JACOB
Hey, hey, hey. It's gonna be all
right. We're in this together,
pal. Okay, I'm gonna help you

out. I'm gonna help you find
Tina, find Queenie, and we'll
all be happy again. Just like
old times.

*He spots a slightly sinister figure on the edge of the cliff: all
black, tattered robes.*

> JACOB
> Who is this guy?

> NEWT
> He's the only way I can
> leave the country without
> documentation. Now, you
> don't suffer from motion
> sickness, do you?

> JACOB
> I don't do well on boats,
> Newt.

A beat.

> NEWT
> You'll be fine.

> PORTKEY TOUT
> Stir your stumps—it leaves in
> one minute!

Confused, JACOB looks around for the conveyance,
ignoring the rusty bucket on the ground.

> PORTKEY TOUT
> Fifty Galleons.

> NEWT
> No, we said thirty.

> PORTKEY TOUT
> Thirty to go to France,
> twenty not to tell anyone I
> seen Newt Scamander leaving
> the country illegally.

Angry, NEWT pays up.

> PORTKEY TOUT
> Price of fame, pal.
>   *(checks watch)*
> Ten seconds.

*NEWT picks up the bucket and holds out his hand
to JACOB.*

> NEWT
> *(to JACOB)*
> Jacob.

> JACOB
> ARGH!

They are pulled away into thin air.

CUT TO:

SCENE 48
EXT. PLACE CACHÉE—DAY

*NEWT and JACOB peer around the corner. A French
POLICEMAN is standing in front of the statue of the
robed woman. JACOB is pale, sweaty, and still clutching
the bucket, which has come in handy.*

> JACOB
> I didn't like that Portkey, Newt.

NEWT
(*absently*)
So you keep saying.
Follow me.

NEWT points his wand at the POLICEMAN.

NEWT

Confundus.

The POLICEMAN lurches as though drunk, blinks, shakes his head, then giggles and ambles off, raising his hat at disconcerted passersby.

NEWT
Come on. That'll wear off in a
few minutes.

NEWT leads JACOB through the statue and into Magical Paris. He puts his case down and points his wand at the street.

NEWT

Appare vestigium.

The tracking spell materializes as a swirl of gold, which illuminates traces of recent magical activity in the square.

NEWT

Accio Niffler!

The case bursts open and a Niffler jumps out.

NEWT

Get looking.

NEWT climbs onto the case and inspects impressions of creatures revealed in the air, while the now-trained adult Niffler sniffs out clues.

NEWT

That's a Kappa. That's a
Japanese water demon—

The Niffler sniffs around some shimmering footsteps. The Niffler has found the place where TINA stood in front of the Zouwu.

NEWT sees a vision of TINA.

NEWT

Tina? Tina!
                    (to Niffler)
What have you found?

He bends down to lick the pavement.

JACOB
(glancing around)
And we're licking the
dirt now.

NEWT puts his wand to his ear and listens to a terrifying
roar. He points his wand to the street.

NEWT

Revelio.

JACOB sees what NEWT is looking at: gigantic paw marks
overlaying everything else.

JACOB
(intensely worried)
Newt . . . what made those?

NEWT
That is a Zouwu. It's a
Chinese creature. They are
incredibly fast and incredibly
powerful. They can travel a
thousand miles in a day . . .
and this one could take you
from one part of Paris to the
next in a single leap.

*The Niffler sniffs around more shimmering footsteps—
another place where TINA stood.*

> NEWT
> Oh, good boy.
> *(intensely worried)*
> Jacob, she was here.
> Tina stood here. She has
> incredibly narrow feet, have
> you noticed?

> JACOB
> Can't say that I have.

NEWT sees a vision of KAMA.

> NEWT
> Then someone came
> towards her.

*NEWT points to a feather from KAMA'S hat, sniffs it, and
looks troubled.*

> NEWT
> *Avenseguim.*

*The feather turns like the needle of a compass, pointing
the way.*

NEWT
Follow that feather.

JACOB
What?

NEWT
Jacob, follow the feather.

JACOB
Follow the feather.

NEWT
(of the Niffler)
Where is he? Ah, *Accio* Niffler.

*The Niffler is carried by the spell back into the case.
NEWT takes the case and dashes off.*

JACOB gestures toward the bucket in his hand.

NEWT
Let go of the bucket!

JACOB drops the bucket and chases after NEWT.

SCENE 49
EXT. PARIS—DAY

Establishing shot.

SCENE 50
EXT. PLACE DE FURSTEMBERG—MORNING

QUEENIE approaches the trees in the middle of the square.
She coughs. The roots of the trees rise up and form a
birdcage elevator around her, which descends into the earth.

SCENE 51
INT. MINISTÈRE DES AFFAIRES MAGIQUES,
MAIN LEVEL—MORNING

QUEENIE descends into the beautiful Art Nouveau
French Ministry of Magic, its domed ceiling patterned with
constellations. QUEENIE approaches reception.

> RECEPTIONIST
> Bienvenue au Ministère des
> Affaires Magiques.

> QUEENIE
> I'm sorry, I don't know what
> you just said at all—

RECEPTIONIST
Welcome to the French
Ministry of Magic. What is
your business, please?

QUEENIE
(loudly and slowly)
I need to speak to Tina
Goldstein, she's an American
Auror working on a case
here—

The RECEPTIONIST flicks through a few pages.

RECEPTIONIST
We have no Tina
Goldstein here.

QUEENIE
No, it's . . . I'm sorry there
must be some sort of mistake.
See, I know she's in Paris, she
sent me a postcard. I brought
it, I can show it to you.
Maybe you can help me find
her here?

QUEENIE reaches for her suitcase, which falls open.

QUEENIE
It's just in here. Oh rabbits!
If you can just wait one
moment! I know it's in here
somewhere. I definitely
packed it. Where is it?

*As the RECEPTIONIST gives a Gallic shrug, a genteel
ELDERLY LADY crosses into the shot behind QUEENIE.
She has a distinctive bag in her hands—we follow her into
the elevator—where ROSIER stands waiting. As the doors
close, the ELDERLY LADY transforms into ABERNATHY
and he pulls out an elaborate box . . .*

SCENE 52
EXT. PARIS BACK STREET—DAY

*QUEENIE stands sadly on the street, holding an umbrella.
Then—a double take—did she just see NEWT and JACOB
hurrying from one side street into another?*

JACOB
Could we at least stop for a

coffee, or like a—

NEWT
Not now, Jacob.

JACOB
I don't know.

NEWT
This way. Come on.

JACOB
Pain au chocolat? Half a
croissant, or like, a bonbon?

NEWT
This way.

*QUEENIE sets off down the street, trotting in her haste to
catch up with NEWT and JACOB.*

*We follow her, drawing ever closer, as she chooses from a
bewildering number of side alleys. So absorbed is she in
trying to follow NEWT and JACOB—she can now "hear"
JACOB'S thoughts.*

QUEENIE
(*calls aloud, joyful*)
Jacob! Jacob?

But he has gone. Exhausted and lonely, QUEENIE drops down to the curb in the rain, deafened by the clamor of the thoughts of those in the crowd around her.

A hand falls onto QUEENIE'S shoulder. She turns, beaming. Her expression turns to puzzlement.

ROSIER
Madame? Tout va bien,
Madame?

SCENE 53
EXT. BIRD MARKET—LATER THAT DAY

CREDENCE and NAGINI walk into shot, looking around. CREDENCE steals birdseed as he passes a stall.

GRIMMSON watches them, unnoticed.

SCENE 54
EXT. RUE PHILIPPE LORAND—SHORTLY AFTERWARD—DAY

CREDENCE and NAGINI peer around the corner at the distant Number Eighteen. A light shines in the attic. A shadow moves in front of it.

> CREDENCE
> *(scared)*
> She's home.

Now he is here, he is rooted to the spot. He dare not proceed. NAGINI prizes his hand from behind his back.

She leads him across the road.

SCENE 55
EXT. REAR OF 18 RUE PHILIPPE LORAND—
MINUTES LATER—DAY

*A door stands open into the yard. They slide through it
into a servants' passageway. NAGINI'S nostrils flare. Her
eyes dart around. There is something wrong. They proceed
toward the stairs.*

SCENE 56
INT. 18 RUE PHILIPPE LORAND, LANDING
OUTSIDE MAID'S ROOM—DAY

*CREDENCE and NAGINI reach the landing. A door
stands ajar. A shadow cast by lamplight: what seems to be a
woman, sewing. The shadow pauses in its work. NAGINI is
edgy, nervous, looking around.*

> IRMA (O.S.)
>> Qui est là?

*CREDENCE can neither move nor speak. NAGINI
realizes this.*

NAGINI
C'est votre fils, madame.

She takes CREDENCE'S hand and pulls him gently into the room. Mended and freshly washed clothing hang from racks on the ceiling. They can see the shadow of a woman. NAGINI'S senses are hyperalert. She can smell danger. The shadow stands.

IRMA
Qui êtes-vous?

CREDENCE
(whispers, terrified)
Are you Irma? Are you . . . ?
Are you Irma Dugard?

No response. They move through the hanging fabric toward her.

CREDENCE
I'm sorry. Your name is on
my adoption paper. Does this
make sense? You gave me to
Mrs. Barebone in New York.

A beat.

*A tiny hand pushes the last piece of fabric aside. There
stands IRMA: half-elf, half-human. CREDENCE'S face
reveals confusion, awful disappointment.*

> IRMA
> *(to CREDENCE)*
> I am not your mother. I was
> only a servant.
> *(smiling)*
> You were such a beautiful
> baby. And you are a beautiful
> man. I have missed you.

*ANGLE ON GRIMMSON, watching them from
a doorway.*

> CREDENCE
> Why didn't they want me?
> But why is your name on my
> adoption paper?

> IRMA
> I took you to Mrs. Barebone
> because she was supposed to
> look after you.

NAGINI'S fear is increasing.

ANGLE ON THE DARK WALL BEHIND SWATHES OF FABRIC.

The perfectly camouflaged GRIMMSON emerges from the wall, raises his wand, aims for the silhouetted figures, and dispatches a Killing Curse that sears through the sheets and clothing, leaving smoldering holes. We hear a body fall. NAGINI screams. CREDENCE'S shadow has vanished.

Grinning, certain of triumph, GRIMMSON slashes away the smoking fabric until he stands facing—

IRMA, dead on the floor, and NAGINI, who backs away from him. Slowly, his grin fading, GRIMMSON looks up at the ceiling. The Obscurus is swirling there like thick black smoke.

In a flash, GRIMMSON conjures a domed Shield Charm around himself and IRMA'S body.

And the Obscurus dives, pelting the Shield Charm like a million bullets, rising and re-forming and diving again, but though the magical barrier trembles, it is not broken.

Now the Obscurus expands in fury, smashing apart the attic like a tornado.

*GRIMMSON smiles up at the Obscurus: We'll meet again.
He Disapparates.*

*Mingling with the debris of the destroyed attic, the
Obscurus slams inward and CREDENCE re-forms. He
stands looking down at the tiny body.*

SCENE 57
EXT. ALLEYWAY—AFTERNOON

*Fresh from IRMA'S murder, GRIMMSON stands in
a covered alleyway beneath a bridge over the Seine.
GRINDELWALD appears.*

> GRIMMSON
> She's dead.

*GRINDELWALD walks toward him and halts when they
are face-to-face.*

> GRINDELWALD
> How did the boy take it?

GRIMMSON
(*shrugging*)
He's sensitive. The Ministry
won't be happy when I tell
them I've missed. They know
my reputation.

GRINDELWALD
Listen to me. The disapproval
of cowards is praise to
the brave. Your name will
be written in glory when
wizards rule the world. And
the clock is ticking faster.
You watch over Credence.
Keep him safe. For the
greater good.

GRIMMSON
For the greater good.

SCENE 58
EXT. PARISIAN CAFÉ—EVENING

*A pair of lovers sit over coffee. NEWT is scanning
every man who leaves the café, checking the reaction of
the feather trapped beneath the glass. JACOB stares at
the lovers.*

> JACOB
> You know what I miss about
> Queenie? Everything. I even
> miss the stuff that drove me
> nuts. Like the mind reading . . .
> *(he notices NEWT'S inattention)*
> . . . I was lucky to have someone
> like her even interested in
> anything I thought. You know
> what I mean?

A beat.

> NEWT
> Sorry?

> JACOB
> I was saying, you're sure
> the guy is here that we're
> looking for?

NEWT
Definitely. The feather says so.

SCENE 59
INT. PARISIAN CAFÉ, BATHROOM—EVENING

A cramped and dirty bathroom. KAMA stares into the mirror, his featherless fedora perched on the tap. Suddenly his face twitches. He raises his bandaged hand to his eye and rubs it, shaking his head. He removes his hand and stares at his reflection. We close in. A tiny tentacle is visible at the corner of his eye. He whimpers in distress and gropes in his suit pocket for a small bottle of bright green liquid, which he drops into his eye with a dropper.

Another whimper of pain as the tentacle withdraws. He looks at his reflection. It seems normal. He puts his hat back on and leaves.

SCENE 60
INT. PARISIAN CAFÉ—EVENING

KAMA leaves the café. The feather points at him. NEWT lets it out and it flies to KAMA'S hat.

> JACOB
> Is that the guy we're
> looking for?

> NEWT
Yes.

NEWT and JACOB jump up to confront him.

> NEWT
> *(to KAMA)*
> Er—bonjour. Bonjour,
> monsieur.

KAMA makes to carry on walking, ignoring NEWT.

> NEWT
> Oh wait, no, sorry. We
> were . . . we were actually
> just wondering if you'd come
> across a friend of ours?

JACOB
Tina Goldstein.

KAMA
Monsieur, Paris is a large city.

NEWT
She's an Auror. When Aurors
go missing, the Ministry
tend to come looking, so . . .
No, now I suppose it would
probably be better if we just
report her absence—

KAMA
(deciding)
She is tall? Dark? Rather—

JACOB   NEWT
—intense?   —beautiful—

JACOB
(hasty, off NEWT'S look)
—Yeah, what I meant to say—
she's very—very pretty—

NEWT
She's intense too.

                    KAMA
I think I saw someone like
this last night. Perhaps if I
showed you where?

                    NEWT
If you wouldn't mind. That
would be lovely.

                    KAMA
Sure.

SCENE 61
INT. KAMA'S HIDEOUT—EVENING

*The interior of KAMA'S hideout is pitch black. The sound
of water dripping. A brief shaft of sunlight reveals TINA,
sleeping lightly on the floor in her coat.*

                    NEWT
        Tina?

*She wakes. A moment as NEWT and TINA stare at each
other. Each has thought of the other daily for a year. With*

no sign of KAMA, it seems she has been rescued.

                    TINA
               (joyful, disbelieving)
          Newt!

*TINA notices KAMA entering in the background and
raising his wand. Her expression changes.*

                    KAMA
          Expelliarmus!

*NEWT'S wand flies out of his hand into KAMA'S. Bars
form across the door, imprisoning them.*

                    KAMA
               (through the door)
          My apologies, Mr. Scamander!
          I shall return and release you
          when Credence is dead!

                    TINA
          Kama, wait!

                    KAMA
          You see, either he dies . . . or
          I do.

He claps a hand to his eye.

> KAMA
> No, no, no, no. Oh no. No,
> no, no.

He jerks convulsively and slides to the floor, unconscious.

> NEWT
> Well, that's not the best start
> to a rescue attempt.

> TINA
> This was a rescue attempt?
> You've just lost me my
> only lead.

JACOB launches for the door, trying to break it down.

> NEWT
> (innocent)
> Well, how was the
> interrogation going before
> we turned up?

*TINA throws him a dark look. She strides to the back of
the cave.*

*Pickett, who, unnoticed, has hopped out of NEWT'S pocket,
successfully picks the lock, and the bars swing open.*

JACOB

Newt!

NEWT

Well done, Pick.
(*to TINA*)
You need this man, you say?

TINA

Yeah. I think this man knows
where Credence is, Mr.
Scamander.

*As they bend over the unconscious KAMA, they hear an
earth-shattering roar from somewhere above them. They
look at each other.*

NEWT

Well, that'll be the Zouwu.

NEWT grabs his wand and Disapparates.

SCENE 62
EXT. PARISIAN BRIDGE—NIGHT

In the middle of the bridge is the Zouwu, terrified and lethal. It is too badly hurt to keep running, but it is swiping at passersby, who are screaming and running out of the way. Cars screech to a halt.

NEWT Apparates in the middle of the bridge, fifty yards from the Zouwu, holding his case. A second later, TINA

Apparates too, holding JACOB'S arm. JACOB is sagging under the weight of the unconscious KAMA.

JACOB
(calls)
Newt, get out of there!

NEWT stoops down slowly and opens his case. The Zouwu snarls, crouches, and begins to advance on NEWT.

Very slowly, so as not to alarm the Zouwu, NEWT lowers his arm into the case, feeling for something. It takes him longer than he expected. Frowning, he reaches deeper inside. The Zouwu advances. It bares its teeth.

NEWT has found what he was looking for. He raises his arm. He is holding a fluffy toy bird on a stick and rope.

A beat. The Zouwu's eyes start to follow the bird.

The Zouwu's tail twitches. It crouches lower than ever. Then, with a sudden bound, it soars through the air toward NEWT. Screams from the onlookers—NEWT will surely be crushed—

But at the last moment he lets the bird fall into the case and the Zouwu sails after it in a flash of rainbow color, python tail flailing and—WHAM—NEWT slams the lid shut.

Uproar from the crowd, sirens approaching, police cars converging on the bridge. FLAMEL'S card flies up out of NEWT'S pocket.

TINA and JACOB, still carrying KAMA, run toward NEWT, and all four Disapparate.

FANTASTIC BEASTS:
THE CRIMES OF GRINDELWALD

SCENE 63
EXT. HOGWARTS—DAY

*An ominous procession of AURORS marches up the drive
toward the castle, among them, THESEUS and LETA.*

*CLOSE ON AN UPPER WINDOW. STUDENTS staring
down at the strangers, nudging one another. The AURORS
enter the school.*

SCENE 64
**INT. DEFENSE AGAINST THE DARK ARTS
CLASSROOM—DAY**

*DUMBLEDORE is teaching. A space in the middle of
the room, all students enjoying the spectacle. A large
boy—McCLAGGAN—is braced for attack, his robes
covered in dust, his tie knotted around his ear. He and
DUMBLEDORE circle each other.*

> DUMBLEDORE
> What were the three biggest
> mistakes that you made last time?

McCLAGGAN
Caught by surprise, sir.

DUMBLEDORE
What else?

McCLAGGAN
Didn't parry before counter-
curse, sir.

DUMBLEDORE
Very good. And the last one . . .
the most important one?

*McCLAGGAN looks away, thinking. DUMBLEDORE
hits him unawares. McCLAGGAN flies into the air,
DUMBLEDORE conjures a sofa, McCLAGGAN hits it
and slides to the floor.*

DUMBLEDORE
Not learning from the
first two.

*The class laughs. The door opens. TRAVERS, THESEUS,
and four other AURORS enter, YOUNG MINERVA
McGONAGALL behind them.*

McGONAGALL
This is a school, you've
no right—

TRAVERS
I'm the Head of Magical Law
Enforcement and I have the
right to go wherever I please.
(to the students)
Out of here.

They don't move.

DUMBLEDORE
(to the students)
Go with Professor
McGonagall, please.

*They file out, curious or alarmed. The last out
is McCLAGGAN.*

McCLAGGAN
(to TRAVERS)
He's the best teacher
we've got.

> DUMBLEDORE
> (*quiet*)
> Thanks, McClaggan.

> TRAVERS
> Get out!

> McGONAGALL
> Come, McClaggan.

The door closes.

> TRAVERS
> Newt Scamander is in Paris.

> DUMBLEDORE
> Really?

> TRAVERS
> Cut the pretense. I know he's
> there on your orders.

> DUMBLEDORE
> If you'd ever had the pleasure
> to teach him, you'd know
> Newt is not a great follower
> of orders.

TRAVERS tosses a small book to DUMBLEDORE, who catches it in one hand.

> TRAVERS
> *(indicating the book)*
> You've read *The Predictions of Tycho Dodonus*?

> DUMBLEDORE
> Many years ago.

> TRAVERS
> *(reads)*
> "A son cruelly banished
> Despair of the daughter
> Return—"

> DUMBLEDORE
> Yes, I know it.

> TRAVERS
> There's a rumor this prediction refers to the Obscurial. They say that Grindelwald wants—

> DUMBLEDORE
> —a highborn henchman. I've heard the rumor.

TRAVERS
And yet Scamander appears
wherever the Obscurial
goes, to protect him.
Meanwhile you have built
up quite a little network of
international contacts—

DUMBLEDORE
(quiet, steely)
However long you keep
me and my friends under
surveillance, you're not going
to discover plots against you,
Travers, because we want
the same thing: the defeat of
Grindelwald. But I warn you,
your policies of suppression
and violence are pushing
supporters into his arms—

TRAVERS
I'm not interested in
your warnings!
(controlling himself)
Now, it pains me to say it,
because—well, I don't like you.

TRAVERS and DUMBLEDORE both chuckle.

> TRAVERS
> But . . . you are the only
> wizard who is his equal. I
> need you to fight him.

A pause. The AURORS watch.

> DUMBLEDORE
> I cannot.

> TRAVERS
> Because of this?

*He casts a spell to show moving pictures of TEENAGE
DUMBLEDORE and TEENAGE GRINDELWALD. The
AURORS are shocked.*

*The TEENAGE DUMBLEDORE and TEENAGE
GRINDELWALD stare intently into each other's eyes.*

> TRAVERS
> You and Grindelwald were as
> close as brothers.

> DUMBLEDORE
> We were closer than brothers.

DUMBLEDORE is looking at the pictures. These memories are agony. He is full of remorse but, almost worse: nostalgia for the only time in his life he felt fully understood.

TRAVERS
Will you fight him?

DUMBLEDORE
(pained)
I can't.

TRAVERS
Then you have chosen
your side.

He flicks his wand once more. Thick metal cuffs— Admonitors—appear on DUMBLEDORE'S wrists.

TRAVERS
From now on, I shall know
every spell you cast. I'm
doubling the watch on you,
and you will no longer
teach Defense Against the
Dark Arts.
(to THESEUS)
Where's Leta? We need to go
to Paris!

He storms out. The AURORS follow. THESEUS is last to the door.

> DUMBLEDORE
> *(quietly)*

Theseus.

THESEUS looks back.

> DUMBLEDORE

Theseus, if Grindelwald calls
a rally, don't try and break
it up. Don't let Travers send
you in there. If you ever
trusted me—

> TRAVERS (O.S.)
> THESEUS!

THESEUS leaves.

SCENE 65
INT. DESERTED HOGWARTS CORRIDOR—DAY

The late afternoon sun falls through the windows as LETA walks along a corridor populated only with memories. She stops beside an open door.

The Great Hall is lit with floating candles.

SCENE 66
INT. EMPTY HOGWARTS CLASSROOM—DAY

LETA walks slowly into the classroom, then turns to look back into the corridor and—

DISSOLVE TO:

SCENE 67
INT. EMPTY HOGWARTS CLASSROOM—
SEVENTEEN YEARS PREVIOUSLY—MORNING

13-YEAR-OLD LETA stands hiding inside the empty classroom while students in cloaks trundle by, pushing trunks and carrying owls. It is the last day of the winter term and nearly everyone is going home.

ANGLE ON TWO 13-YEAR-OLD GRYFFINDOR GIRLS pushing trunks.

> GRYFFINDOR GIRL 1
> You know she stays here
> every vacation. Her family
> don't actually want her home.

> GRYFFINDOR GIRL 2
> I don't blame them, she's
> so annoying. Even the
> name Lestrange makes me
> feel sick—

LETA flings herself into their path, pointing her wand.

> 13-YEAR-OLD LETA
> *Oscausi!*

GRYFFINDOR GIRL 2'S mouth is sealed shut as though she never had one. Triumphant, LETA flees the scene, pushing past shocked students.

> GRYFFINDOR GIRL 1
> *(screams)*
> Professor McGonagall!
> LESTRANGE HAS DONE
> IT AGAIN!

> McGONAGALL (O.S.)
> Lestrange, stop running!
> LESTRANGE! Disobedient
> children. Stop! Shame on
> the House of Slytherin.
> One hundred points! Two
> hundred! Get back here, right
> now! Stop! Stop it! Stop it!
> You stop it! Get back here!

> GRYFFINDOR GIRL 1
> Miss, it was Lestrange.
> She's horrible—

McGONAGALL silences the girl.

ANGLE ON LETA, sprinting around a corner.

She wrenches open a side door and plunges inside.

SCENE 68
INT. HOGWARTS CUPBOARD—SEVENTEEN YEARS PREVIOUSLY—MORNING

13-YEAR-OLD LETA slams the door and stands there, ear against it. She hears running, distant shouts. Then a sound behind her makes her jump and turn around.

13-YEAR-OLD NEWT is already in occupation of the cupboard. He has hidden a couple of tanks here, one containing tadpoles, another Streelers. A lined cardboard box serves as a nest for the raven chick he is cradling in his hand. It wears a splint on its broken leg. NEWT and LETA stare at each other.

> 13-YEAR-OLD LETA
> Scamander . . . why aren't
> you packing?

> 13-YEAR-OLD NEWT
> I'm not going home.

> 13-YEAR-OLD LETA
> Why not?

> 13-YEAR-OLD NEWT
> *(of the raven)*
> He needs me. It was hurt.

LETA takes in the tanks, then the ugly little bird, to which NEWT now feeds an earthworm.

> 13-YEAR-OLD LETA
> What is that?

> 13-YEAR-OLD NEWT
> A raven chick.

She is mildly intrigued now.

> 13-YEAR-OLD LETA
> The raven's my family's
> emblem.

She watches him stroking the bird's head. As he places the chick gently in her hands, she seems to see him plainly for the first time.

DISSOLVE TO:

SCENE 69
INT. DEFENSE AGAINST THE DARK ARTS
CLASS—FOURTEEN YEARS PREVIOUSLY—DAY

It is Boggart time. DUMBLEDORE supervises the line
of teenagers advancing to try their luck. "Riddikulus"—
"Riddikulus"—gusts of hilarity as a shark becomes a
flotation device, a zombie's head turns into a pumpkin, a
vampire turns into a buck-toothed rabbit.

> DUMBLEDORE
> All right, Newt. Be brave.

16-YEAR-OLD NEWT moves to the front of the queue.
The Boggart turns into a Ministry desk.

> DUMBLEDORE
> Mmm, that's an unusual one.
> So Mr. Scamander fears what
> more than anything else in
> the world?

> 16-YEAR-OLD NEWT
> Having to work in an office, sir.

The class roars with laughter.

> DUMBLEDORE
> Go ahead, Newt.

> 16-YEAR-OLD NEWT
> *Riddikulus!*

NEWT turns the desk into a gamboling wooden dragon and moves aside.

> DUMBLEDORE
> Well done. Good job.

It is 16-YEAR-OLD LETA'S turn, but she doesn't move. She is terrified.

> DUMBLEDORE
> *(kind, to LETA)*
> Leta, it's only a Boggart, it
> can't hurt you. Everyone's
> scared of something.

A group of girls stands together, enjoying her fear.

> GRYFFINDOR GIRL 1
> I've been looking forward
> to this.

LETA steps forward. The Boggart transforms and at once, all laughter is extinguished. Green light is reflected on every horrified face.

We see a shadow, with a tiny human hand. LETA lets out a sob and runs from the room.

SCENE 70
EXT. HOGWARTS LAKE, BOWTRUCKLE ISLAND—FOURTEEN YEARS PREVIOUSLY— EVENING

NEWT finds LETA sitting by the lake, tearstained, eyes swollen. They look at each other.

16-YEAR-OLD LETA
I don't want to talk about it!

He holds out his hand and she lets him pull her up. He leads her past a few trees until they reach the one where Bowtruckles are climbing and fighting and playing. They freeze at the humans' approach but relax when they recognize NEWT. He holds out a finger. One of them jumps on.

16-YEAR-OLD NEWT
They know me, or they'd
hide. They only nest in trees
with wand-quality wood, did
you know that?
(beat)
And they have very complex
social lives. If you watch
them for long enough, you
realize . . .

He trails off. She is watching him, not the Bowtruckles.
NEWT reaches across to her, the Bowtruckle standing on
his wrist. His hand grazes hers.

DUMBLEDORE (V.O.)
Hello, Leta.

DISSOLVE TO:

SCENE 71
INT. EMPTY HOGWARTS CLASSROOM—
AFTERNOON

LETA is still sitting at her old desk in the present-day classroom. DUMBLEDORE enters.

> DUMBLEDORE
> This is a surprise.

> LETA
> *(cold)*
> Finding me in a classroom?
> Was I such a bad student?

> DUMBLEDORE
> On the contrary, you were
> one of my cleverest.

> LETA
> I said bad, not stupid. Don't
> bother answering. I know
> you never liked me.

> DUMBLEDORE
> Well, you're wrong. I never
> thought you bad.

LETA
You were alone, then.
Everybody else did.
(very quietly)
And they were right. I
was wicked.

A beat as he considers her.

DUMBLEDORE
Leta, I know how painful the
rumors about your brother
Corvus must be for you.

LETA
No, you don't. Not unless you
had a brother who died too.

DUMBLEDORE
In my case, it was my sister.

She stares at him, both hostile and curious.

LETA
Did you love her?

DUMBLEDORE
Not as well as I should have done.

He steps toward LETA.

> DUMBLEDORE
> It's never too late to free
> yourself. Confession is
> a relief, I'm told. A great
> weight lifted.

She stares at him. What does he know—or suspect?

> DUMBLEDORE
> *(sotto voce)*
> Regret is my constant
> companion. Do not let it
> become yours.

SCENE 72
INT. GRINDELWALD'S HIDEOUT, DRAWING ROOM—END OF DAY

QUEENIE is on the sofa, beside a table of tea and cakes. She sets down her empty teacup. We feel her slight awkwardness as it is instantly refilled by ROSIER.

QUEENIE

Oh, no, thank you. You've
been real kind, but my sister
Tina's probably worried sick
about me, you know. Banging
on all the doors and things, so
I think I'd better be going.

ROSIER

But you haven't met your host.

QUEENIE
(a little wistfully)
Oh, are you married?

ROSIER
(smiling)
Let's say . . . deeply committed.

QUEENIE
(innocent)
You see, I can't tell if you're
making a joke or if you're
just . . . French.

*ROSIER laughs and leaves. QUEENIE is confused. An
enchanted teapot hovering in midair nudges her, intent on
refilling her cup.*

QUEENIE
(to the teapot)
Hey, knock it off.

*The door opens. GRINDELWALD enters. QUEENIE
stands and the teapot and cups smash to the ground. She
draws her wand and aims it at GRINDELWALD.*

QUEENIE
You stay right there. I know
what you are.

He walks slowly toward her.

GRINDELWALD
Queenie, we are not here
to hurt you. We only want
to help you. You're so
very, very far from home.
Far away from everything
you love. Everything that
was comfortable.

QUEENIE stares, keeping her wand raised.

GRINDELWALD
I would never see you harmed,
ever. It is not your fault that

your sister is an Auror. I wish
you were working with me
now towards a world where
we wizards are free to live
openly, and to love freely.

GRINDELWALD'S hand touches her wand-tip and
lowers it.

GRINDELWALD
You are an innocent. So go
now. Leave this place.

SCENE 73
INT. HOGWARTS, ROOM OF REQUIREMENT—NIGHT

*A spartan room. A large object stands against the wall,
covered in black velvet. DUMBLEDORE stands thinking
for a moment, then approaches the covered object and pulls
the curtain down.*

The Mirror of Erised is revealed. He has not looked into it for many years. Bracing himself, he now does so.

We see TEENAGE DUMBLEDORE and TEENAGE GRINDELWALD facing each other in a barn. Both score their palms with their wands. Now bleeding, they interlace their hands . . .

DUMBLEDORE turns his head away, fighting the impulse to cover the glass again.

Bracing himself, he looks up.

From their bloody palms rise two glowing drops of blood, which mingle and merge to create one. A metal shape begins to form around the droplet, becoming more defined and intricate. It is GRINDELWALD'S vial.

The vision fades and the present-day GRINDELWALD stands smiling out of the mirror, surrounded by blackness.

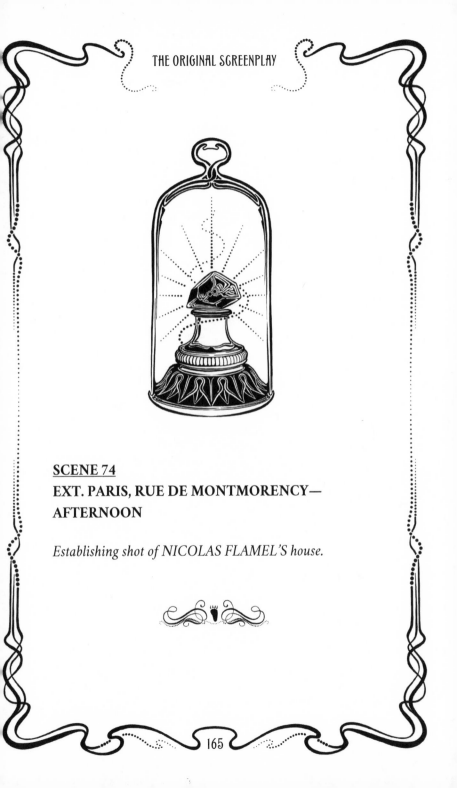

SCENE 74
EXT. PARIS, RUE DE MONTMORENCY—
AFTERNOON

Establishing shot of NICOLAS FLAMEL'S house.

SCENE 75
INT. FLAMEL HOUSE—AFTERNOON

A creepy medieval drawing room. The tapestries sport moving figures and odd runes. A large crystal ball in a corner shows dark clouds. TINA is trying to wake up KAMA with a bottle of smelling salts. He moves slightly. The Predictions of Tycho Dodonus slips out of his pocket onto the floor. TINA picks it up and opens it to the prediction KAMA has underlined.

NEWT'S case is open on a table. The Zouwu roars from inside. TINA turns to look at it, listening.

SCENE 76

INT. NEWT'S CASE, ZOUWU ENCLOSURE—
AFTERNOON

*A wild Chinese habitat. NEWT is curled up in dense
undergrowth. The Zouwu picks him up and dangles him
from a claw.*

<u>SCENE</u> 77
INT. FLAMEL HOUSE—AFTERNOON

JACOB enters and sees TINA watching the case. She hastily looks back at the book.

> JACOB
> *(calling into case)*
> Hey, Newt, buddy. Tina's
> up here. She's all by her
> lonesome and maybe you
> want to come up and keep
> her company?
> *(beat)*
> I've been looking for food,
> and I ain't found any. I guess
> I'm gonna go upstairs and try
> my luck in the—I dunno—
> the attic!

SCENE 78
INT. NEWT'S CASE, ZOUWU ENCLOSURE—
AFTERNOON

Still dangling from the Zouwu's claw, NEWT soothes and coaxes her until he can reach her harness and remove it. The Zouwu is finally freed from her chains.

> NEWT
> You're all right.

> JACOB (O.S.)
> Okay!

SCENE 79
INT. FLAMEL HOUSE—AFTERNOON

JACOB is about to leave when NEWT clambers back out of the case.

> NEWT
> She's responded well to the
> Dittany. She was born to

run, you see. I think she's just
lacking in confidence—

He glances at TINA. She pockets The Predictions of
Tycho Dodonus *and speaks, not quite looking at NEWT.*

TINA

Mr. Scamander, have you
got anything in your case
that might help revive this
man? I need to question
him. I think he knows who
Credence really is. The
scars on his hand suggest an
unbreakable vow—

NEWT
(eager, overlapping)
—unbreakable vow. Yeah, I
noticed that too—

They examine the unconscious KAMA.

NEWT

Lumos.

*NEWT'S and TINA'S hands brush as NEWT advances his
lit wand-tip to look in KAMA'S eye. Both jump. NEWT*

stares into KAMA'S eye. The tiny flicker of a tentacle,
swiftly withdrawn—

> TINA
> *(gasps)*
> What was that?

> NEWT
> *(serious)*
> There must be a water
> dragon in that sewer—they
> carry these parasites, you see.
> They . . . Jacob?

> JACOB
> Yeah?

> NEWT
> In my case, in the pocket
> there, you'll find a pair
> of tweezers.

> JACOB
> Tweezers?

> NEWT
> They're thin and pointy—

TINA
Thin, little pointy things.

JACOB
Yes, I know what tweezers are.

NEWT
(to TINA)
You might not want to watch
this . . .

TINA
I can handle it.

*NEWT succeeds in catching and pulling at the tentacle in
KAMA'S eye.*

NEWT
Come on. You're all right.
Jacob, will you take that
for me?

*He has extracted something like a spindly, waterborne
spider, which he hands to JACOB.*

JACOB
Ew! Calamari.

KAMA has started muttering, distraught, semiconscious.

KAMA
I must kill him . . .

TINA
Who? Credence? Who—?

NEWT
It may take him a few hours
to recover. The parasite's
poison is quite strong.

TINA
I'll have to go to the Ministry
with what I've got.
    (a wobble in her voice)
It was nice to see you again,
Mr. Scamander.

*She strides from the room, leaving NEWT perplexed
and upset.*

SCENE 80
INT. FLAMEL HOUSE, HALLWAY—AFTERNOON

JACOB follows TINA into the hall.

> JACOB
> Hey, hold on one second, will
> you? Well, hold on! Wait! Tina!

She leaves. As the front door closes, NEWT appears at the drawing room door.

> JACOB
> (to NEWT)
> You didn't mention
> salamanders, did you?

> NEWT
> No, she just—ran. I don't
> know . . .

> JACOB
> (firm)
> So you chase after her!

NEWT grabs his case. He leaves.

SCENE 81
EXT. RUE DE MONTMORENCY—END OF DAY

TINA is hurrying up the road. NEWT hastens to catch up.

> NEWT
> Tina. Please, just listen to me—

> TINA
> Mr. Scamander, I need to
> go talk to the Ministry—
> and I know how you feel
> about Aurors—

> NEWT
> I may have been a little strong
> in the way that I expressed
> myself in that letter—

> TINA
> What was the exact phrase? "A
> bunch of careerist hypocrites"?

> NEWT
> I'm sorry, but I can't admire

people whose answer to
everything that they fear or
misunderstand is "kill it"!

TINA
I'm an Auror and I don't—

NEWT
Yes, and that's because you've
gone middle head!

TINA
(stopping)
Excuse me?

NEWT
It's an expression derived
from the three heads of the
Runespoor. The middle one
is the visionary. Every Auror
in Europe wants Credence
dead—except you. You've
gone middle head.

A beat.

TINA
Who else uses that expression,

Mr. Scamander?

NEWT considers.

> NEWT
> I think it might just be me.

All lights are extinguished as every building is wrapped in black banners.

Muggles pass, totally immune, but a YOUNG RED-HAIRED WITCH nearby is walking along. She, like NEWT and TINA, can see the banners.

TINA steps into the middle of the road, watching the black silk fall out of the sky to shroud the surrounding buildings in darkness.

> TINA
> It's Grindelwald. He's calling
> his followers.

We pan up one length of flowing black silk until we achieve an aerial view of Paris. The entire city is being covered in GRINDELWALD'S dark banners.

SCENE 82
EXT. WIZARDING CAFÉ—END OF DAY

Witches and wizards hurrying outside to see what is invisible to Muggle passersby.

SCENE 83
EXT. PARISIAN STREET—END OF DAY

QUEENIE reaches out to the nearest black banner, and an emblem of a white raven appears beneath her touch.

SCENE 84
EXT. PLACE DE FURSTEMBERG—END OF DAY

NEWT still following TINA. They stand surrounded by the impressive scale of GRINDELWALD'S banners.

> TINA
> It's too late. Grindelwald's
> come for Credence. He might
> already have him.

> NEWT
> *(suddenly forceful)*
> It's not too late. We can still get
> to him first.

He grabs her hand and pulls her on.

> TINA
> Where are you going?

> NEWT
> The French Ministry of Magic.

TINA

That's the last place Credence
would go!

NEWT

There's a box hidden at the
Ministry safe. It's a box that can
tell us who Credence really is.

TINA

A box? What are you talking
about?

NEWT

Trust me.

SCENE 85
EXT. DERELICT BUILDING, ROOFTOP—LATE
AFTERNOON

*CREDENCE is breaking up birdseed and feeding it to a
small chick when NAGINI appears behind him.*

NAGINI
(urgently)

Credence.

She leads him back through the open window, out onto the roof. The Eiffel Tower is visible behind them.

We pan around and see GRINDELWALD sitting on the rooftop near them both.

GRINDELWALD

Shh.

CREDENCE
(whispers)

What do you want?

GRINDELWALD

From you? Nothing. For you?
Everything I never had. But
what is it you want, my boy?

CREDENCE

I want to know who I am.

GRINDELWALD

This is where you will find
proof of your true identity.

GRINDELWALD takes a piece of parchment from his
pocket and throws it into the air. The parchment flutters to
CREDENCE and lands gently in his hand.

GRINDELWALD
Come to Père Lachaise tonight
and you will discover the truth.

He bows, then Disapparates, leaving CREDENCE holding
a map of Père Lachaise cemetery.

SCENE 86
INT. FLAMEL HOUSE—END OF DAY

An uncomfortable JACOB is asleep in a chair beside the semiconscious KAMA. KAMA is muttering.

> KAMA
> Father . . . why did you make
> me . . . ?

JACOB jolts awake as if from a bad dream.

> JACOB
> Wait! Wait—

Now fully awake, JACOB'S stomach begins to rumble.

A figure appears behind JACOB. Six-hundred-year-old NICOLAS FLAMEL stands at the entrance to his alchemist's studio.

> FLAMEL
> I'm afraid we keep no food in
> the house.

JACOB yelps in fear.

> JACOB
> (terrified)
> Are you a ghost?

> FLAMEL
> (amused)
> No, no, I am alive, but
> I am an alchemist, and
> therefore immortal.

JACOB
You don't look a day over
three-seventy-five. Hey, sorry
we didn't knock—

FLAMEL
No matter. Albus told me
some friends might be
dropping in.
    (holding out his hand)
Nicolas Flamel.

JACOB
Oh. Jacob Kowalski.

*They shake hands. JACOB'S grip is firm—too firm for the
alchemist's fragile bones.*

FLAMEL
Ooh!

JACOB
I'm sorry.

FLAMEL
It's all right.

JACOB
I didn't—

FLAMEL looks over at the large crystal ball, in which dark billowing clouds and flashes of lightning have appeared.

> FLAMEL
> Aha! At last, we see developments!

> JACOB
> *(drawing closer)*
> I've seen one of these before.
> It was at the fair. There was
> this dame there, and she had
> a veil. I gave her a nickel and
> she told me about my future.
> *(beat)*
> She missed out on quite a bit,
> actually.

We close in on the orb, into dark billowing smoke and flashes of lightning, into the center where we see CREDENCE—

> JACOB (O.S.)
> Hey—wait a minute! I
> know him. That's that kid.
> That's Credence—

—and then it becomes the Lestrange tomb, its stone raven prominent. Suddenly, QUEENIE appears inside the tomb,

sitting on a stone bench, waiting . . .

>   JACOB
>   Hey! That's Queenie! There
>   she is.
>   *(as if to QUEENIE)*
>   Hi, baby!
>   *(to FLAMEL)*
>   Where is this? Is this—is
>   this here?

>   FLAMEL
>   This is the Lestrange tomb.
>   It lies in the cemetery of Père
>   Lachaise. . .

>   JACOB
>   *(to QUEENIE in the
>   crystal ball)*
>   I'm coming, baby. Stay
>   right there—
>   *(to FLAMEL)*
>   Thank you, thank you,
>   Mr. Flamel!

JACOB clutches FLAMEL'S hands in gratitude.

FLAMEL

Ahh!

JACOB

Oh no. I'm sorry! I'm sorry,
okay?

FLAMEL

Ouch.

JACOB

Oh—look after Mr. Tentacles
for me.

*He turns. The sofa is empty. JACOB runs out of the
room into the hall. The front door stands open. KAMA
has escaped.*

JACOB

Oh no. I'm sorry, I gotta go.

FLAMEL

Please, you must not go to
the cemetery!

But JACOB too runs off into the night.

BACK TO FLAMEL.

*He has shuffled after JACOB, but on realizing he is gone,
FLAMEL turns anxiously back to the orb. Black flames are
swirling around it.*

*FLAMEL shuffles back into his studio and opens a
cupboard. We glimpse glass vials, tubes, and the glowing
Philosopher's Stone. He heaves from a shelf a padlocked
book embossed with a phoenix. He touches the padlock and
it springs open.*

CLOSE ON THE BOOK as he flicks through it.

*Each page holds a photograph captioned with a name.
FLAMEL turns the pages, but the subjects of all the pictures
are missing.*

> FLAMEL
>> Oh dear—

DUMBLEDORE'S portrait is blank.

*FLAMEL flicks open another page. EULALIE HICKS, a
young American professor at Ilvermorny, looks around,
worried.*

> EULALIE
>> What's happening?

FLAMEL
Exactly what he said would
happen. Grindelwald rallies
tonight at the cemetery, and
there will be death!

EULALIE
Then you gotta go!

FLAMEL
(*panicked*)
What? I haven't seen action in
two hundred years . . .

EULALIE
You can do this, Flamel. We
believe in you.

SCENE 87
EXT. PLACE DE FURSTEMBERG—DAY

*TINA and NEWT stand in a nearby alleyway, looking out
over the square where tree roots previously rose to form the
birdcage elevator to the French Ministry.*

NEWT
The box is in the ancestral
records room, Tina. So, three
floors down.

*NEWT rummages in his pockets and pulls out a tiny bottle
with only a couple of muddy drops left inside it.*

TINA
Is that Polyjuice?

NEWT
(of the bottle)
Just enough to get me inside.

*He looks down at his coat and finds one of THESEUS'S
hairs on his shoulder. He adds it to the mixture, drinks, and
turns into THESEUS, still wearing NEWT'S clothes.*

TINA
Who—?

NEWT
My brother, Theseus. He's an
Auror. And a hugger.

SCENE 88
INT. MINISTÈRE DES AFFAIRES MAGIQUES,
MAIN LEVEL—NIGHT

THESEUS exits a meeting room and strides toward LETA, who is waiting for him.

> LETA
> What's happening?

> THESEUS
> Grindelwald's rallying. We
> don't know where, but we
> think it's tonight.

LETA and THESEUS kiss.

> LETA
> Be careful.

> THESEUS
> Of course.

> LETA
> Promise me you'll be careful.

> THESEUS
> Of course, I'm going to be

careful. Listen, I want you to
hear this from me. They think
that Credence boy might be
your missing brother.

LETA
My brother is dead. He died.
How many times, Theseus?

THESEUS
I know, I know. And the
records, the records will prove
that, okay? They can't lie.

TRAVERS
(*sharply*)
Theseus.

THESEUS leaves LETA and joins TRAVERS.

TRAVERS
I want every person at that
rally arrested. If they resist—

THESEUS
Sir—forgive me . . . but if we
go in too heavy, don't we run
the risk of adding to the—

TRAVERS
Just do it.

THESEUS catches sight of NEWT-AS-THESEUS and TINA walking, heads down, through the Ministry typing pool. The brothers' eyes meet.

ANGLE ON NEWT-AS-THESEUS AND TINA.

NEWT-AS-THESEUS grabs TINA'S arm and makes a sharp turn down a corridor. THESEUS sets off in pursuit, leaving LETA and the angry TRAVERS (who hasn't spotted NEWT) behind. LETA backs away from the throng and slips through a side door.

SCENE 89
INT. MINISTÈRE DES AFFAIRES MAGIQUES, CORRIDOR—NIGHT

NEWT-AS-THESEUS and TINA run along a corridor lined with pictures, the Polyjuice Potion already wearing off NEWT.

NEWT

I don't suppose you can
Disapparate on Ministry
premises in France, can you?

TINA

No.

NEWT

Pity.

The Potion wears off completely.

TINA

Newt!

NEWT

Yes, I know. I know there's—

*At once, every portrait along the corridor turns into
NEWT. An alarm sounds.*

ALARM (O.S.)

Urgence! Urgence! Un sorcier
suivi, Newt Scamander, est
entré dans le Ministère!
Emergency! Emergency!
A tracked wizard, Newt

Scamander, has entered the
Department of Magic!

THESEUS moves into shot.

> THESEUS
>
> Newt!

> TINA
> *(running)*
> That's your brother?

> NEWT
> Yes—I think I may
> have mentioned in my
> letters we have quite a
> complicated relationship—

> THESEUS
> NEWT, STOP!

*NEWT and TINA sprint through a second door,
which leads—*

SCENE 90

INT. MINISTÈRE DES AFFAIRES MAGIQUES, MAILROOM—NIGHT

—into a mailroom. Two elderly PORTERS are pushing mailcarts across the circular room.

> TINA
> Does he want to kill you?

> NEWT
> Frequently.

> THESEUS
> No!

As they sprint past the mailcarts, THESEUS sends a curse after them, sending the mailcart boxes flying. TINA blocks the spell.

> TINA
> He needs to control
> his temper!

TINA points her wand. THESEUS is slammed down into a high chair that TINA has conjured out of nowhere. Hands bound, THESEUS flies backward on the chair into a meeting room, where he slams into a wall.

NEWT
(awed)
I think that might have been
the best moment of my life.

TINA laughs. NEWT and TINA sprint on.

SCENE 91
INT. LESTRANGE MAUSOLEUM—NIGHT

An ancient tomb containing many sarcophagi is dominated by the grand marble tomb of LETA'S father.

ABERNATHY and MACDUFF enter carrying the bag retrieved from the French Ministry and remove the elaborate box, which they plant in the mausoleum to be found.

SCENE 92
EXT. PÈRE LACHAISE CEMETERY—SHORTLY AFTERWARD—NIGHT

JACOB is panting as he runs through the dark, deserted cemetery, looking for the tomb he saw in the orb. A faint light in the distance shows him the Lestrange mausoleum.

SCENE 93
EXT. LESTRANGE MAUSOLEUM—A MINUTE LATER—NIGHT

JACOB reaches the tomb. A stone raven on the lintel.

JACOB
(whispers)

Queenie?

No answer. He enters.

SCENE 94
INT. LESTRANGE MAUSOLEUM—NIGHT

ANGLE ON JACOB entering a small space full of shadows and sarcophagi. A single lamp.

> JACOB
> Queenie, honey?

> MALE WIZARD
> Don't. Don't move.

A movement behind him. He whirls around. A silhouetted figure lunges at him.

SCENE 95
INT. MINISTÈRE DES AFFAIRES MAGIQUES, RECORDS ROOM ATRIUM—NIGHT

NEWT and TINA turn a corner into a beautiful atrium

*area in front of towering Art Nouveau doors carved to
resemble trees. A very old woman behind a desk bars the
way: MELUSINE.*

> MELUSINE
> Puis-je vous aider?

> NEWT
> Er—yes, this is Leta
> Lestrange. And—I'm her—

> TINA
> Fiancé.

*An increased awkwardness between them as MELUSINE
lifts an ancient book onto the desk and opens it.*

*CLOSE ON MELUSINE'S WIZENED FINGER as it
runs down a list of surnames beginning with L.*

> MELUSINE
> *(pointing them on)*
> Allez-y.

> TINA
> *(whispering)*
> Merci.

NEWT
(*sotto voce, behind TINA*)
Thank you.

NEWT grabs TINA'S hand and pulls her toward the doors into the records room. MELUSINE eyes them suspiciously.

NEWT
Tina, about that fiancée business—

TINA
(*brittle*)
Sorry, yeah. I should have
congratulated you—

The doors to the records office open. They enter briskly.

SCENE 96
INT. MINISTÈRE DES AFFAIRES MAGIQUES, RECORDS ROOM—NIGHT

The doors close behind them, plunging them into darkness.

> NEWT

No, that's—

> TINA

Lumos.

An extraordinary acre of shelves stretches away from them, all carved to look like trees, so that they seem to be on the edge of the forest. Pickett pokes his head out of NEWT'S pocket and squeals in excitement.

> TINA

Lestrange.

Nothing happens.

TINA sets off, NEWT right behind her. They weave in and out of the carved shelves bearing rolls of parchment, the occasional prophecy, other mysterious trunks and boxes.

> NEWT

Tina—about Leta—

> TINA

Yes, I've just said, I am happy
for you—

NEWT
Yeah, well, don't.

She stops. Looks at him. What?

NEWT
Please don't be happy.
(*in trouble*)
Uh, no, no. I'm sorry. I
don't . . . Uh, obviously, I—
Obviously I want you to be.
And I hear that you are now.
Uh, which is wonderful.
Sorry—
(*a gesture of hopelessness*)
What I'm trying to say is, I
want you to be happy, but
don't be happy that I'm
happy, because I'm not.
(*off her confusion*)
Happy.
(*off her continued
confusion*)
Or engaged.

TINA
What?

NEWT
It was a mistake in a stupid
magazine. My brother's
marrying Leta, June the
sixth. I'm supposed to be
best man. Which is sort of
mildly hilarious.

TINA
Does he think you're here to
win her back?
(beat)
Are you here to win her back?

NEWT
No! I'm here to—

A beat. He stares at her.

NEWT
—you know, your eyes
really are—

TINA
Are what?

NEWT
I'm not supposed to say.

Pickett is climbing out of NEWT'S pocket onto the nearest shelf. NEWT doesn't notice.

A beat. In a rush:

TINA	NEWT
Newt, I read your book, and did you—?	I still have a picture of you—wait, did you read—?

NEWT pulls the picture of her from his breast pocket and unfolds it. She is inordinately touched. He looks from the picture to TINA.

> NEWT
> I got this—I mean, it's just
> a picture of you from the
> paper, but it's interesting
> because your eyes in
> newsprint . . . See, in reality
> they have this effect in
> them, Tina . . . It's like fire in
> water, in dark water. I've only
> ever seen that—
>   *(struggling)*
> I've only ever seen that in—

TINA
(whispers)
Salamanders?

A loud bang as the doors to the records room fly open. They jump apart. Somebody has entered the room. They draw back among the shelves.

TINA
Come.

ANGLE ON LETA in the doorway.

She walks inside, desperate. This is her last chance to hide evidence about Corvus's death. The doors close behind her. She raises her wand.

LETA
Lestrange.

The shelves begin to move.

ANGLE ON MELUSINE, watching through the records room doors.

ANGLE ON NEWT AND TINA.

The giant trees are shifting all around them. They are

almost crushed as the Lestrange "tree" flies toward them.
They hop onto a shelf.

ANGLE ON LETA.

The towering stack stops, swaying, in front of her. She
stares. An empty shelf confronts her. A mark in the dust
where a box sat, a slip of parchment in its place.

She picks up the slip and reads it aloud.

> LETA
> "Records moved to Lestrange
> family tomb at Père
> Lachaise."

She spots Pickett hiding among the deed boxes on the shelf.

> LETA
> Circumrota.

The record tower turns, revealing NEWT and TINA
clinging to the shelves.

> LETA
> Hello, Newt.

NEWT

Hello, Leta.

TINA
(*awkwardly, but kindly*)

Hi.

At that moment, MELUSINE enters the records room surrounded by growling Matagots.

NEWT

Oh no.

LETA
(*scared*)

What kind of cats are those?

NEWT

These aren't cats, they're
Matagots. They're spirit
familiars. They guard the
Ministry—but they won't
hurt you unless you—

Panicking, LETA fires a spell at one of the cats.

LETA

Stupefy!

Her spell not only fails, it causes the Matagots to multiply
and become even more aggressive.

NEWT
UNLESS YOU ATTACK THEM!

As each batch of Matagots is hit, they multiply and mutate.
The situation has become dangerous.

LETA

Oops.

NEWT

Leta!

LETA climbs over the balustrade to join NEWT and TINA
on the shelf stack.

LETA

Reverte!

The towering stack flies backward as the Matagots pounce
in a terrifying ebony surge of teeth and claws.

The other "trees" of the records room forest spin and move
as NEWT, TINA, and LETA run through the room chased
by the attacking Matagots.

But just as the Matagots seemingly lose the trail, all of the records room towers retract into the floor, leaving the room empty. The Matagots prowl toward where their prey must surely be standing, only to find—

NEWT'S case.

ANGLE ON THE CASE from above.

A beat.

An explosion as the Zouwu bursts out of the case, NEWT clinging to its back. Roaring, it rears, slashing at the rising tide of Matagots, its mane flashing.

NEWT

Accio!

NEWT'S case flies into his hand.

For a few seconds the Zouwu and NEWT vanish under the seething mass of cats. They fight them off, the Zouwu's immense power unmatched, red tail swishing.

NEWT points his wand at the ceiling.

NEWT

Ascendio!

*The towers rise once again from the floor, lifting NEWT
and the Zouwu high up into the air. Still fighting off the
Matagots as the stacks tip and fall beneath the sheer weight,
the Zouwu clambers across to the balcony.*

SCENE 97
INT. MINISTÈRE DES AFFAIRES MAGIQUES,
MAIN LEVEL—A MINUTE LATER—NIGHT

*The Matagots give chase as the Zouwu gallops out of
the room, leaving injured and thwarted Matagots in its
wake. The Zouwu carves a path of destruction through the
Ministry. It takes one last leap over the typing pool . . .*

*. . . and its immense magical power propels it up and out
through the glass roof.*

SCENE 98
EXT. PÈRE LACHAISE CEMETERY—NIGHT

NEWT and the Zouwu land in the cemetery. With one gigantic leap, the Zouwu has taken them to freedom.

The few Matagots that have followed them growl and then shrink. Reduced to the size of domestic cats in the Muggle environment, they "meow" pitifully.

NEWT opens his case as the Zouwu nudges him with affection.

NEWT

> Whoa, whoa, whoa. Okay, wait.
> Hold it there, please. Come on.
> All right, okay, wait. Okay.

LETA and TINA climb out of the case to observe NEWT coaxing the Zouwu.

TINA shakes the cat bird toy she has retrieved from the case. The Zouwu's eyes light up.

Unnoticed by NEWT and TINA, LETA runs away into the darkness.

SCENE 99
INT. LESTRANGE MAUSOLEUM—A MINUTE LATER—NIGHT

LETA enters the ornate space lined with sleeping statues of dead Lestranges. JACOB stands backed against the wall next to NAGINI in snake form, who is repeatedly lashing out at KAMA, who is trying to get a clean shot at CREDENCE.

> KAMA
> *(to NAGINI)*
> Move back! Move! Out of the
> way! If I must kill you as well
> as Corvus, I shall!

LETA raises her wand at KAMA, who swings round to see her, wand pointed at him—a standoff.

> LETA
> Stop!

She walks forward, stricken but determined, at last, to do the right thing. KAMA is mesmerized. She is his mother reborn. He moves toward LETA, studies her face in the darkness, transfixed and moved by the sight of her.

LETA
Yusuf?

KAMA
Is that really you? My little
sister . . . ?

*NEWT and TINA enter and exchange looks—another piece
of the puzzle.*

CREDENCE
(to LETA)
So he's your brother? Who
am I?

LETA
I don't know.

He pushes past LETA and faces KAMA, unprotected.

CREDENCE
I'm tired of living with no
name and no history. Just tell
me my story—then you can
end it.

KAMA
Your story is our story . . .
      (*gesturing to LETA*)
Our story.

LETA
No, Yusuf—

KAMA
      (*determined*)
My father was Mustafa
Kama, a pureblood of
Sénégalese descent and most
accomplished.

SCENE 100
EXT. PARK—1896—DAY

We see a beautiful woman, LAURENA, dressed in an
exquisite gown, walking through a park with her husband,
MUSTAFA—clearly in love. A YOUNG YUSUF by
their side.

KAMA (V.O.)
My mother, Laurena, was
equally high-bred—a noted
beauty. They were deeply
in love. They knew a man
of great influence, from a
famous French pureblood
family. He desired her.

*Watching from a distance, an intense wizard, CORVUS
LESTRANGE SR., studies her beauty.*

SCENE 101
INT. KAMA MANSION—1896—NIGHT

*LAURENA'S gown changes to a nightdress. She is walking
slowly downstairs, a supernatural wind blowing.*

KAMA (V.O.)
Lestrange used the Imperius
Curse to seduce and abduct
her . . .

The twelve-year-old KAMA runs after his mother, tugs at her hand, and tries to pull her back upstairs. She throws him off. The front door flies open. LESTRANGE SR. stands at the foot of the garden path. LAURENA walks toward him. KAMA chases after her. LESTRANGE SR. points his wand at KAMA and sends him sprawling.

LAURENA lies on the bed as IRMA carries a newborn swaddled in a blanket to LESTRANGE SR.

SCENE 102
INT. LESTRANGE MAUSOLEUM—NIGHT

> KAMA
> . . . that was the last time I
> ever saw her. She died, giving
> birth to a little girl.
> > *(to LETA)*
> You.

Tears start in LETA'S eyes, reliving the guilt she holds.

KAMA

The news of her death drove
my father insane. With his
dying breath, my father
charged me to seek revenge.
(*determined*)
Kill the person Lestrange
loves best in the world . . . I
thought at first it would be
easy . . . he had only one close
relative . . . you. But—

LETA

Say it . . .

KAMA

. . . he never loved you.

SCENE 103
INT. LESTRANGE MANOR, BEDROOM—1901—
DAY

We reenter the story to find LESTRANGE SR. with a new,

blond wife.

> KAMA (V.O.)
> He remarried not three
> months after her death. He
> loved her no more than he
> had loved you . . . But then . . .

IRMA takes the BABY BOY who has just been born, and
passes him to LESTRANGE SR., who is delighted.

> KAMA (V.O.)
> . . . his son, Corvus, was born
> at last. And that man who had
> never known love was filled
> with it . . .

SCENE 104
INT. LESTRANGE MAUSOLEUM—NIGHT

CREDENCE looks on, rapt—is this who he is? He's hungry
to know more.

                    KAMA
          All he cared about was
          little Corvus.

A beat.

                    CREDENCE
          So. . . this is the truth? I am
          Corvus Lestrange?

          KAMA   LETA
          Yes.   No.

CREDENCE stares from one to the other.

KAMA turns and looks at LETA. Her eyes are unfocused.
These memories have haunted her nightmares for years.

                    KAMA
                  (to LETA)
          Realizing that Mustafa
          Kama's son had sworn
          revenge, your father sought
          to hide you where I couldn't
          find you. So he confided you
          to his servant, who boarded a
          ship for America.

LETA
He did send Corvus to
America, but—

KAMA
His servant, Irma Dugard,
was a half-elf. Her magic
was weak and therefore left
no trace I could follow. I
had only just discovered
how you had escaped when
I received news I never
expected . . . The ship had
gone down at sea . . . But you
survived, didn't you?
(to CREDENCE)
Somehow, someone had
pulled you from the water!
"A son cruelly banished
Despair of the daughter
Return, great avenger
With wings from the water."
There—
(points at LETA)
—stands the despairing
daughter. You are the
winged raven returned
from the sea, but I—I am the

avenger of my family's ruin.

KAMA raises his wand.

> KAMA
> I pity you, Corvus, but you
> must die.

> LETA
> Corvus Lestrange is already
> dead. I killed him.

LETA raises her wand.

> LETA
>
> *Accio!*

A heavy box, hidden in the corner of the mausoleum, comes crashing to her through the dust. A series of clicks as cogs whirr . . . Puzzle-like, it falls apart.

> LETA
> My father owned a very
> strange family tree. It only
> recorded the men . . .

We glimpse a tree with an orchid-like flower twisting around it.

LETA
. . . the women in my family
were recorded as flowers.
Beautiful. Separate.

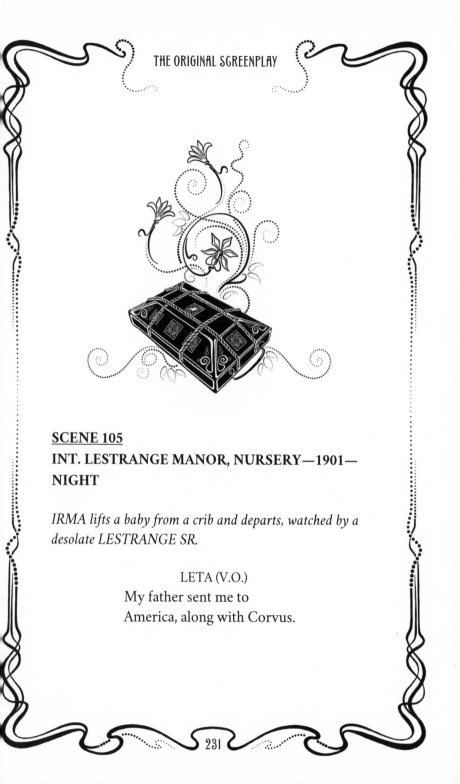

<u>SCENE 105</u>
INT. LESTRANGE MANOR, NURSERY—1901—NIGHT

IRMA lifts a baby from a crib and departs, watched by a desolate LESTRANGE SR.

> LETA (V.O.)
> My father sent me to
> America, along with Corvus.

<u>SCENE 106</u>
INT. SHIP'S CABIN—1901—NIGHT

*IRMA is asleep, CHILD LETA awake on a lower bunk,
and BABY CORVUS screaming in his crib.*

> LETA (V.O.)
> Irma was to pose as a
> grandmother with two
> grandchildren . . .

*The lights suddenly flicker on and off—CHILD LETA
hasn't moved, she is still looking at the screaming BABY
CORVUS.*

> LETA (V.O.)
> Corvus never stopped crying.

*In the background there is a commotion as figures run
along the corridor outside the door. As CHILD LETA
approaches BABY CORVUS, who continues to cry,
IRMA wakes. She goes to investigate the fuss and noise in
the corridor.*

> LETA (V.O.)
> I never wanted to hurt him.

CHILD LETA is transfixed by the baby.

> LETA (V.O.)
> I only wanted to be free of
> him. Just for a moment . . .

SCENE 107
INT. SHIP'S CORRIDOR—1901—NIGHT

The door of the opposite cabin is ajar. BABY CREDENCE is inside, fast asleep. CHILD LETA slips inside. She swaps the babies.

> LETA (V.O.)
> Just a single moment.

SCENE 108
INT. SHIP'S CABIN—1901—NIGHT

CHILD LETA enters with BABY CREDENCE.

>   IRMA
>   Give him to me!

The ship lurches again. IRMA snatches BABY CREDENCE, not noticing the switch amid the confusion. The cabin door bangs open to reveal a dark-haired young woman wearing a nightdress and life jacket.

>   CREDENCE'S AUNT
>   Irma? They want us to put on
>   life jackets!

She slips and slides into her own cabin and picks up BABY CORVUS, also not realizing the babies have been switched.

SCENE 109
EXT. LIFEBOAT—1901—NIGHT

*CHILD LETA, IRMA, and BABY CREDENCE are in
one boat, CREDENCE'S AUNT and BABY CORVUS in
another.*

*A huge wave is approaching. CHILD LETA watches as
the lifeboat bearing CREDENCE'S AUNT and BABY
CORVUS is overturned.*

*CLOSE ON THE SURFACE OF THE WATER. A few
survivors reappear, including CREDENCE'S AUNT, but
not BABY CORVUS . . . CREDENCE'S AUNT pulls off
her life jacket so she can dive too . . .*

*She does not reemerge. We close in through the surface
of the water, past the drowning woman, and see the dark
shape of a drowning baby trailing bubbles of magical light
as he sinks . . . and his figure becomes . . .*

SCENE 110
INT. LESTRANGE MAUSOLEUM—NIGHT

. . . the drowning baby falling through sea-green light,
hanging in the air in the mausoleum. LETA has conjured it.
It has haunted her all her life and now she shows it to them.

The orchid representing LETA on the Lestrange family tree
twists around the branch labeled CORVUS LESTRANGE *until*
the leaves wither and die.

> NEWT
> You didn't mean to do it,
> Leta. So it wasn't your fault.

> LETA
> Oh, Newt. You never met a
> monster you couldn't love.

A long look between them, a look full of memories.

> TINA
> Leta, do you know who
> Credence really is? Did
> you know, when you
> swapped them?

                    LETA
        No.

CREDENCE reacts.

An opening suddenly appears in the wall of the mausoleum.
All stare at the steps leading down into the earth. The sound
of a gigantic crowd rumbles beneath them.

                    JACOB
        Queenie?

Before anyone can stop him, he runs down the steps.
NEWT and TINA dash after him. LETA looks at KAMA,
then follows NEWT.

KAMA hurries after her.

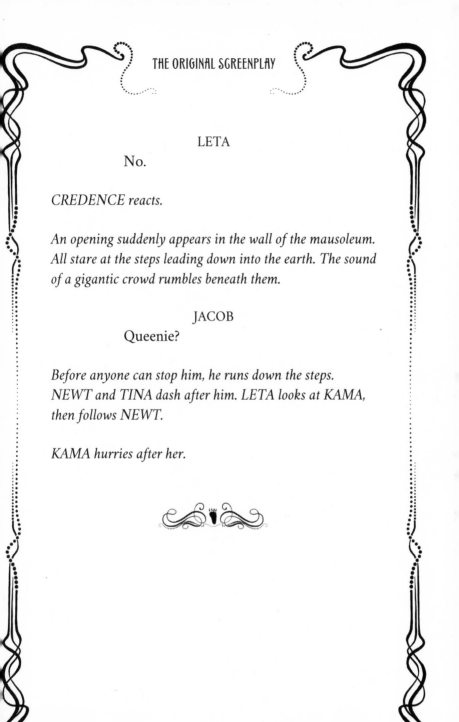

<u>SCENE 111</u>
INT. UNDERGROUND AMPHITHEATER—NIGHT

JACOB steps out of the narrow staircase into an underground amphitheater and is confronted by a terrifying sight.

Thousands of witches and wizards mill around, some already seated on stone benches. The atmosphere is edgy. Some are nervous but curious. Others excited, still others ready for a fight. Masked ACOLYTES steward the crowd.

ANGLE ON CREDENCE AND NAGINI entering the amphitheater.

Awed and intimidated by the sight, they are swept along in the swell of people moving deeper into the auditorium.

NAGINI tries to hold CREDENCE back.

> NAGINI
> They're purebloods. They kill
> the likes of us for sport!

He carries on walking. NAGINI hesitates, then follows too.

*Looking around, JACOB spots a familiar blond head—
QUEENIE, being accompanied to a front row seat by
an ACOLYTE.*

> JACOB
> *(whispers)*
>
> Queenie.

He pushes his way into the crowd.

ANGLE ON JACOB running toward QUEENIE.

She turns. Utter delight—

> QUEENIE
> Jacob! Honey, you're here! Hi!

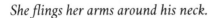

She flings her arms around his neck.

> QUEENIE
> *(reading his mind)*
> Oh, honey, I'm so sorry, I
> never should have done it, I
> love you so much—

> JACOB
> And you know that I love
> you, right?

> QUEENIE
> Yeah.

> JACOB
> Good, now let's get the hell
> out of here.

*He tries to pull her back the way he came, but she tugs
him back.*

> QUEENIE
> *(serious)*
> Oh, wait. Wait a second. I
> just thought maybe we could
> hear him first. You know, just
> listen, that's all.

JACOB
What are you talking about?

*She pulls a confused JACOB into a seat beside her in
the front row, clutching his hand. JACOB looks around
nervously at all the purebloods.*

ANGLE ON NEWT AND TINA.

*They are already in the crowd, TINA looking around for
those they have followed, but NEWT, perturbed, is starting
to see the bigger picture.*

TINA
It's a trap.

NEWT
Yeah. Queenie—the family
tree—it's all been bait.

*He looks around. ACOLYTES are moving to cover all
the entrances.*

TINA
We have to find a way out of
here, right now.

NEWT
You go find the others.

TINA
What are you gonna do?

NEWT
I'll think of something.

He sets off. She moves more slowly into the crowd, looking for JACOB and CREDENCE.

ANGLE ON AN ACOLYTE watching NEWT'S progress.

The lights dim. The crowd begins to cheer.

SCENE 112
INT. UNDERGROUND AMPHITHEATER—NIGHT

We follow GRINDELWALD onstage as the audience explodes with delight. Their hysteria builds as he stands there, part demagogue, part rock star.

ANGLE ON TINA, edging through the crowd, searching.

She spots QUEENIE and, at a short distance, CREDENCE. Whom should she approach first? She chooses CREDENCE, but as she moves, is blocked by an ACOLYTE. They make eye contact. TINA knows she is wildly outnumbered. Under the ACOLYTE'S gaze, she sinks onto a bench.

We pan over the crowd. We see QUEENIE, rapt, and JACOB, low in his seat and scared ... KAMA, who is skeptical ... CREDENCE, transfixed, and NAGINI, who trusts nobody ... LETA, studying GRINDELWALD, wondering ...

ANGLE ON GRINDELWALD, gesturing at the crowd to settle.

> GRINDELWALD
> My brothers, my sisters, my
> friends: the great gift of your
> applause is not for me.
> *(off noises of denial)*
> No. It is for yourselves.

ANGLE ON LETA, amid the crowd. She is not clapping, but she feels the pull of GRINDELWALD'S charisma.

GRINDELWALD
You came today because of
a craving and a knowledge
that the old ways serve us no
longer . . . You come today
because you crave something
new, something different.

ANGLE ON CREDENCE, listening.

GRINDELWALD
It is said that I hate Les Non-
Magiques. The Muggles. The
No-Maj. The Can't-Spells.

Jeers and hisses from much of the crowd. JACOB sinks
deeper into his seat. QUEENIE is momentarily anxious;
she seizes his hand: No, wait, listen—

GRINDELWALD
I do not hate them. I do not.

Silence from the crowd.

GRINDELWALD
For I do not fight out of
hatred. I say the Muggles
are not lesser, but other.

Not worthless, but of other
value. Not disposable, but of a
different disposition.
   (beat)
Magic blooms only in rare
souls. It is granted to those
who live for higher things.
Oh, and what a world
we could make, for all of
humanity. We who live for
freedom, for truth—

His eyes meet QUEENIE'S in the front row.

     GRINDELWALD
—and for love.

We pan across QUEENIE, now heart and soul his . . .

SCENE 113
EXT. PÈRE LACHAISE CEMETERY—NIGHT

The figures of fifty AURORS appear in silhouette among the mausoleums. We move in and see that THESEUS is one of them.

>   THESEUS
>   It isn't illegal to listen to him!
>   Use minimum of force on the
>   crowd. We mustn't be what
>   he says we are!

But on other faces we see nervousness, even fear, and on a few, a clear will to fight, to avenge.

SCENE 114
INT. UNDERGROUND AMPHITHEATER—
NIGHT

BACK TO GRINDELWALD onstage.

>   GRINDELWALD
> The moment has come to
> share my vision of the future
> that awaits if we do not rise

up and take our rightful place
in the world.

*ROSIER appears onstage. Bowing, she presents the skull-
hookah to GRINDELWALD.*

*Total silence falls in the auditorium. GRINDELWALD
is illuminated by the skull's golden light. He inhales
deeply through the tube. His eyes roll up into his head. He
exhales . . .*

*. . . and it is extraordinary. A gigantic Technicolor cloak
seems to unfurl from his lips across the high stone ceiling,
bearing moving images—the crowd gasps—*

*Thousands of marching, booted feet . . . explosions, men
running with guns . . .*

*CLOSE ON THE FACES OF THE CROWD, mesmerized
and afraid, the light of the vision playing across their faces.*

CLOSE ON NEWT, stunned.

*The vision of a nuclear blast rocks the amphitheater. It is
horrifying. The crowd feels it, is terrified. Screams, until the
vision subsides, leaving murmurs of panic . . .*

CLOSE ON JACOB, horrified.

> JACOB
> Not another war . . .

The vision fades. All eyes return to GRINDELWALD.

> GRINDELWALD
> That is what we are fighting!
> That is the enemy—their
> arrogance, their power lust,
> their barbarity. How long will
> it take before they turn their
> weapons on us?

We pan around the exits and see AURORS, unnoticed, entering the auditorium, fanning out among the crowd.

CLOSE ON THESEUS, who is worried: The situation is volatile and could go badly wrong.

The crowd settles, agitated, expectant. They are waiting for some new, extraordinary revelation.

> GRINDELWALD
> Do nothing when I speak of
> this. You must remain calm
> and contain your emotions.

(beat)
There are Aurors here
among us.

*Gasps. Heads turn. We see the AURORS looking around in
panic. They are wildly outnumbered. The crowd is hostile.*

GRINDELWALD
*(to the AURORS who
have just entered)*
Come closer, brother
wizards! Join us.

*To mounting hisses and angry jeers, the AURORS know they
have no choice but to walk forward and show themselves.*

ANGLE ON LETA, turning to look.

She spots THESEUS. A long, charged look between them.

THESEUS
(to the other AURORS)
Do nothing. No force.

*But one of the jumpiest young AURORS has made eye
contact with the YOUNG RED-HAIRED WITCH. She is
angry, as twitchy as he is, fingering her wand.*

GRINDELWALD
They have killed many of
my followers, it is true. They
caught and tortured me in
New York. They had struck
down their fellow witches
and wizards for the simple
crime of seeking truth, for
wanting freedom . . .

*He is deliberately playing on the unstable YOUNG RED-
HAIRED WITCH'S feelings. The YOUNG AUROR
raises his wand a few inches. He can sense her desire
for violence—*

GRINDELWALD
Your anger—your desire for
revenge—is natural.

*And it happens. She raises her wand, but the YOUNG
AUROR curses first. To the horror of her companions, she
falls, dead.*

GRINDELWALD
No!

*Screams fill the auditorium. GRINDELWALD ascends
into the crowd, which parts for him. He kneels and pulls the
YOUNG RED-HAIRED WITCH'S limp body into his arms.*

GRINDELWALD
(to her friends)
Take this young warrior back
to her family.

*The Niffler, unnoticed, wriggles out from beneath
GRINDELWALD'S boot and disappears into the crowd.*

GRINDELWALD
Disapparate. Leave. Go forth from
this place and spread the word: It
is not we who are violent.

*They take the body and Disapparate, as does most of the
crowd. THESEUS and the AURORS watch the purebloods
leave. THESEUS ushers his AURORS forward.*

THESEUS
(looking at GRINDELWALD)
Let's take him.

*They start to descend the amphitheater steps.
GRINDELWALD turns his back on the advancing
AURORS, relishing the fight to come.*

GRINDELWALD
Protego diabolica.

He spins and draws a protective circle of black fire around himself. The exits close.

ABERNATHY, CARROW, KRAFFT, MACDUFF, NAGEL, and ROSIER walk through the flames into the circle.

ANGLE ON KRALL, hesitating.

Then he decides the circle is the better option, braces himself, runs into the fire—and is consumed.

> GRINDELWALD
> Aurors, join me in this circle,
> pledge to me your eternal
> allegiance, or die. Only here
> shall you know freedom, only
> here shall you know yourself.

GRINDELWALD sends a wall of flames into the air, pursuing fleeing AURORS.

> GRINDELWALD
> Play by the rules! No
> cheating, children.

NAGINI grabs CREDENCE and tries to drag him away with her, but he is staring at GRINDELWALD.

CREDENCE
He knows who I am.

NAGINI
He knows what you were
born, not who you are . . .

GRINDELWALD smiles at CREDENCE through the fire.

NEWT
Credence!

*NEWT tries to fight the fire but it becomes more monstrous,
lashing out with eel-like spurs.*

*CREDENCE decides: Pulling free of NAGINI, he walks
toward the flames.*

*Devastated, NAGINI is forced back by the ever-
expanding fire.*

*ANGLE ON QUEENIE AND JACOB, who are pressed up
against a different stretch of wall.*

JACOB
Queenie. You gotta wake up.

QUEENIE
(*a decision*)
Jacob, he's the answer. He
wants what we want.

JACOB
No, no, no, no, no, no.

QUEENIE
Yeah.

JACOB
No.

The black flames are coming toward them, fast.

ANGLE ON CREDENCE, walking through the flames.

GRINDELWALD embraces him like a prodigal son.

GRINDELWALD
This has all been for you,
Credence.

ANGLE ON QUEENIE AND JACOB.

QUEENIE
Walk with me.

JACOB
Honey, no!

QUEENIE
(*screams*)
Walk with me!

JACOB
You're crazy.

She reads his mind, turns, hesitates, then walks into the black fire.

JACOB
(*desperate, disbelieving*)
No! Queenie, don't do it!

She screams, and JACOB covers his face, terrified, as she passes through the ring of fire and joins GRINDELWALD'S side.

JACOB
Queenie . . .

TINA
QUEENIE!

QUEENIE Disapparates.

TINA retaliates, throwing a curse at GRINDELWALD,
but the circle of fire lashes out in ever more violent spears.
GRINDELWALD conducts the flames as though leading
an orchestra, the Elder Wand his baton, as the forks of fire
strike at AURORS attempting to Disapparate or flee.

Half a dozen AURORS lose their heads and run through
the flames to GRINDELWALD.

ANGLE ON NEWT AND THESEUS, standing together
on the amphitheater steps.

> GRINDELWALD
> Mr. Scamander. Do you think
> Dumbledore will mourn for
> you?

GRINDELWALD throws a large burst of black fire
at them both, and THESEUS and NEWT defend
themselves.

> LETA (O.S.)
> Grindelwald! Stop!

GRINDELWALD catches sight of LETA.

> THESEUS
> Leta . . .

GRINDELWALD
This one I believe I know.

THESEUS makes a gigantic effort of will, carving a passage toward LETA, determined to reach her. They are using all their skill to keep the flames at bay.

GRINDELWALD moves toward her through the flames as THESEUS fights closer, desperate to reach her.

GRINDELWALD
Leta Lestrange . . . despised
entirely amongst wizards . . .
unloved, mistreated . . . yet
brave. So very brave.
(to LETA)
Time to come home.

He stretches out his hand. She contemplates it.

He looks at her, eyes narrowed.

She looks toward both THESEUS and NEWT, who are watching her, stunned.

LETA
I love you.

*She points her wand at the skull in ROSIER'S hands,
which explodes. ROSIER is knocked backward and
GRINDELWALD is momentarily obscured in a whirl
of chaos.*

LETA
(to the others)
GO! GO!

*The fire engulfs LETA. THESEUS goes wild. He tries to
dive after her.*

*But NEWT grabs him and they Disapparate. The fire,
mirroring GRINDELWALD'S rage, explodes, chasing them.*

GRINDELWALD
(whispers)
I hate Paris.

SCENE 115
EXT. PÈRE LACHAISE CEMETERY—A MINUTE
LATER—NIGHT

NEWT and THESEUS, TINA with JACOB, and KAMA
with NAGINI all Apparate out from the amphitheater.
The black fire pursues them like a many-headed hydra,
erupting out of every mausoleum.

FLAMEL arrives at last.

The cemetery is on the verge of destruction. The fire
GRINDELWALD has unleashed is out of control. It forms
dragon-like creatures intent on annihilation.

> FLAMEL
> TOGETHER! In a circle, your
> wand into the earth, or all
> Paris will be lost!

> NEWT & THESEUS
> *Finite!*

> TINA
> *Finite!*

> KAMA
> *Finite!*

FLAMEL

Finite!

Our heroes, minus JACOB, make a circle, plunge their wands into the earth.

It takes almost superhuman power to contain GRINDELWALD'S demonic fire, which they are forced to combat with flames still more deadly. United, our heroes fight . . .

And at last, their purifying fire drives GRINDELWALD'S back. The entrances to the underground lair are sealed.

They have saved the city.

FLAMEL comforts JACOB. NAGINI sits in the darkness, tearful.

NEWT shuffles over awkwardly to the bereft THESEUS. NEWT hesitates, struggling to find words of comfort. Then, for the first time in his life, he puts his arms around his brother. They hug.

NEWT

I've chosen my side.

The Niffler hobbles over to NEWT, who picks him up . . .

NEWT
(to the Niffler)
Come on. Yeah. No,
you're okay.

. . . then notices GRINDELWALD'S vial in its paws. He takes the pendant, amazed. NEWT tucks both the vial and Niffler inside his coat.

SCENE 116
EXT. THE VIADUCT AT HOGWARTS—DAWN

DUMBLEDORE is walking across the viaduct from Hogwarts, toward NEWT, JACOB, TINA, THESEUS, NAGINI, KAMA, TRAVERS, and assorted AURORS, who stand at the other end.

NEWT walks ahead alone to meet DUMBLEDORE. TRAVERS moves to stop him.

THESEUS
(to TRAVERS)
I think it's best if he
speaks to him alone.

TRAVERS opens his mouth to protest. Meets THESEUS'S gaze. Nods curtly.

NEWT walks along toward DUMBLEDORE. They meet in the middle of the viaduct.

SCENE 117
EXT. AUSTRIA, NURMENGARD CASTLE WINDOW—DAWN

CREDENCE is staring out at the sky, scared of what he has done but awed by the magnificent vista. We pan out to see Nurmengard, high on its mountain.

SCENE 118
INT. NURMENGARD CASTLE, SIDE ROOM—DAWN

GRINDELWALD and QUEENIE are watching

*CREDENCE through the half-open door into a grand
drawing room.*

> GRINDELWALD
> (*whispers*)
> Is he frightened of me still?

> QUEENIE
> (*whispers*)
> You need to be careful . . .
> He's not sure he made the
> right choice. Be very gentle
> with him.

*She smiles as he bows her out through a separate door.
Once he is sure she has gone, he walks into the drawing
room to join CREDENCE.*

> GRINDELWALD
> I have a gift for you, my boy.

*From behind his back he takes a handsome wand. With
a bow, he presents it to CREDENCE, who cannot believe
his eyes.*

<u>SCENE 119</u>
EXT. THE VIADUCT AT HOGWARTS—DAY

*We see that DUMBLEDORE is hollow-eyed. His usual
calm has gone. He's a man at the end of his tether.*

> DUMBLEDORE
> Is it true about Leta?

NEWT nods.

> NEWT
> Yes.

DUMBLEDORE
I'm so sorry.

*NEWT pulls out the vial. DUMBLEDORE stares at it,
simultaneously tormented and amazed.*

NEWT
It's a blood pact, isn't it? You
swore not to fight each other.

Bitterly ashamed, DUMBLEDORE nods.

DUMBLEDORE
(overcome)
How in the name of Merlin
did you manage to get . . . ?

*The Niffler pokes its head out of NEWT'S jacket, sad to see
the pendant go.*

NEWT
Grindelwald doesn't seem
to understand the nature of
things he considers simple.

DUMBLEDORE raises his hands to show the Admonitors.

CLOSE ON THESEUS.

He raises his wand.

BACK TO DUMBLEDORE AND NEWT.

The Admonitors fall from DUMBLEDORE'S wrists.

The vial—blood troth—hangs in the air between them.

> NEWT
> Can you destroy it?

> DUMBLEDORE
> Maybe . . . maybe.

Overcome, tearful, he tries to speak cheerfully.

> DUMBLEDORE
> (of the Niffler)
> Would he like a cup of tea?

They turn to walk back toward Hogwarts.

> NEWT
> He'll have some milk. Hide
> the teaspoons.

The others walk slowly after them.

SCENE 120
INT. NURMENGARD CASTLE—DAWN

> GRINDELWALD
> You have suffered the most
> heinous of betrayals, most
> purposely bestowed upon
> you by your own blood. Your
> own flesh and blood. And
> just as he has celebrated your
> torment, your brother seeks
> to destroy you.

*CREDENCE inhales sharply. His chick steps gingerly onto
GRINDELWALD'S palm. GRINDELWALD throws it in
the air, where it catches alight.*

> GRINDELWALD
> There is a legend in your
> family that a phoenix will
> come to any member who is
> in dire need.

Given room at last, the bird stretches its wings and becomes

full size. The bird is aflame, a phoenix reborn.

> GRINDELWALD
> It is your birthright, my boy.
> As is the name I now restore
> to you.
>> *(whispers)*
> Aurelius. Aurelius
> Dumbledore.

CREDENCE turns. The power of his Obscurus can at last be channeled. He points the wand at the window and a spell of immense power shatters the glass and breaks apart the mountain opposite.

CREDENCE stands staring through the shattered glass at his handiwork. He is extraordinary, and this is just his beginning.

THE
END

GLOSSARY OF FILM TERMS

Angle on—The camera focuses on a particular character or object

Back to—The camera returns to a particular character or action within a scene, after focusing on another

Close on—The camera films a person or object from close range

Cut to—Move to another scene with no transition

Dissolve—A transition between scenes in which one image gradually fades out while another fades in to take its place

Ext.—*Exterior*; an outdoor location

Int.—*Interior*; an indoor location

O.S.—*Off-screen*; action that takes place off-screen or dialogue that is spoken without seeing the character on-screen

Pan—Camera movement involving the camera turning on a stationary axis moving slowly from one subject to another

POV—*Point-of-view*; the camera films from a particular character's point of view

Sotto voce—Spoken at a whisper or under one's breath

V.O.—*Voice-over*; dialogue spoken by a character not present in the scene on-screen

CAST & CREW

Warner Bros. Pictures Presents
A Heyday Films Production
A David Yates Film

FANTASTIC BEASTS:
THE CRIMES OF GRINDELWALD

Directed by..David Yates

Written by...J.K. Rowling

Produced by ....David Heyman, p.g.a., J.K. Rowling, p.g.a.,
Steve Kloves, p.g.a., Lionel Wigram, p.g.a.

Executive Producers .... Tim Lewis, Neil Blair,
Rick Senat, Danny Cohen

Director of Photography .... Philippe Rousselot, A.F.C./ASC

Production Designer... Stuart Craig

Editor...Mark Day

Costume Designer... Colleen Atwood

Music... James Newton Howard

ABOUT THE AUTHOR

J.K. Rowling is the author of the much-loved series of seven Harry Potter novels, originally published between 1997 and 2007. Along with the three companion books written for charity, the series has sold over 500 million copies, been translated into over 80 languages, and made into eight blockbuster films.

Originally written by J.K. Rowling in aid of Comic Relief as a Hogwarts textbook, *Fantastic Beasts and Where to Find Them* became the inspiration behind a new and original five-film series for Warner Bros., the first of which was released in 2016. The second film in the series, *Fantastic Beasts: The Crimes of Grindelwald,* was released in November 2018.

J.K. Rowling has collaborated with playwright Jack Thorne and director John Tiffany on a stage play, *Harry Potter and the Cursed Child*, which opened on London's West End in 2016, on Broadway in 2018, and will have further worldwide openings in 2019.

J.K. Rowling also writes the Cormoran Strike crime novels, under the pseudonym Robert Galbraith. The fourth in this series was published in fall 2018. The Strike books have been adapted for television for BBC and HBO television by Bronte Film & Television. J.K. Rowling is also the author of *The Casual Vacancy*, a stand-alone novel for adults, published in 2012.

ABOUT THE BOOK DESIGN

This book was designed and illustrated by London-based design studio MinaLima. Its founders, Miraphora Mina and Eduardo Lima, were the graphic designers on both *Fantastic Beasts* films and all eight films in the Harry Potter series. Their work has been influential in shaping the visual style of the Wizarding World: from film production to theme park graphics, and bestselling published works.

The cover and illustrations in this book were based on elements and creatures in the story. Its 1920s Art Nouveau rendering echoes the aesthetic of the film and retains an ongoing theme from J.K. Rowling's screenplay *Fantastic Beasts and Where to Find Them*, also designed by MinaLima.

The illustrations were drawn by hand and finished in Adobe Photoshop.

The text was set in Crimson Text and the display type was set in Sheridan Gothic SG.

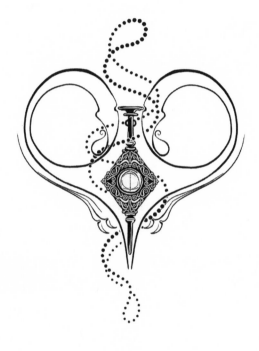